What people are saying about …

D1232280

THE PASTOR'S KID

"Kermit thinks it isn't easy being green; he should try being a pastor's kid. Few roles are more tricky and taxing than growing up as the son or daughter of a minister. And few voices are more qualified to speak to that enigma than Barnabas Piper. *The Pastor's Kid* is an insightful and winsome look at what it means to follow Jesus in a pressurized fishbowl of expectations and is laced with helpful advice to stay sane in the midst of it all. I wish I had had this book to help me make sense of life in my formative years."

Jonathan Merritt, proud PK and author
of *Jesus Is Better Than You Imagined*

"Barnabas Piper challenges us to put faith into action. Practical and insightful, *The Pastor's Kid* is a must-read for anyone who wants a closer relationship with Christ."

Ryan Shook, author of *Firsthand: Ditching
Secondhand Religion for a Faith of Your Own*

"As a PK, I know few understand the perspective from inside the church fishbowl. Barnabas Piper captures the fishbowl perspective and writes what a lot of us PKs have been thinking for a long time. But this book isn't just for PKs. It's for the church. *The Pastor's Kid* is a case study on the effects of unrealistic expectations; those others place on us and the ones we place on ourselves. Every churchgoer should read this book."

Sam S. Rainer, III, a PK raising more PKs

"The tragic celebrity culture that shrouds pastors and their families is a bit like applauding the tallest miniature horse. God is supposed to be the only one we make much of, not the pastor or his children. And yet our need for idols has placed a crushing weight on PKs so that they are, in the words of Barnabas Piper, *known of* and not *known*. As a PK myself I know all too well the euphoria of being known of and the utter emptiness of not being known. This book gives much-needed hope to families navigating the 'reality show' called church. Thank you, Barnabas Piper!"

Bryan Loritts, lead pastor, Fellowship Memphis, and author of *Right Color/Wrong Culture*

THE
PASTOR'S
KID

THE PASTOR'S KID

Finding Your Own Faith and Identity

BARNABAS PIPER

David C Cook

transforming lives together

THE PASTOR'S KID
Published by David C Cook
4050 Lee Vance View
Colorado Springs, CO 80918 U.S.A.

David C Cook Distribution Canada
55 Woodslee Avenue, Paris, Ontario, Canada N3L 3E5

David C Cook U.K., Kingsway Communications
Eastbourne, East Sussex BN23 6NT, England

The graphic circle C logo is a registered trademark of David C Cook.

The website addresses recommended throughout this book are offered as a
resource to you. These websites are not intended in any way to be or imply an
endorsement on the part of David C Cook, nor do we vouch for their content.

Unless otherwise noted, all Scripture quotations are taken from The
Holy Bible, English Standard Version® (ESV®), copyright © 2001 by
Crossway, a publishing ministry of Good News Publishers. Used by
permission. All rights reserved. Scripture quotations marked KJV are
taken from the King James Version of the Bible. (Public Domain.)

LCCN 2014938971
ISBN 978-0-7814-1035-9
eISBN 978-1-4347-0794-9

© 2014 Barnabas Piper

The Team: Alex Field, Karen Lee-Thorp, Ingrid Beck, Amy Konyndyk, Karen Athen
Cover Design: Nick Lee

Printed in the United States of America
First Edition 2014

2 3 4 5 6 7 8 9 10

070214

To Karsten, Ben, Abraham, and
Talitha—my siblings.
Your roads are different than mine; so are your stories.
All of us have had and will have our own
struggles and twists on our way.
Each of you has inspired me and fed these pages.
Thank you, and I love you all.

CONTENTS

FOREWORD

You will ask, "Was it painful for me to read this book?" The answer is yes. For at least three reasons. First, it exposes sins and weaknesses and imperfections in me. Second, it is not always clear which of its criticisms attach to me and the church I love. Third, this is my son, and he is writing out of his own sorrows:

> Writing this book has been hard. Maybe it's more accurate to say that a lot of hardship went into writing this book, some of it in my own family and some of it through the pain of other PKs I connected with along the way. So many PKs carry so much pain and anger and sorrow with them. Some of them have fallen into bitterness, and others are rightly doing the hard work of trust in Jesus to help them through.

I am overwhelmingly thankful that Barnabas is in that last category. It took trust and courage to write this book. The road has been hard. And sometimes, as he says, "We need to pour out what is boiling in us." When that happens, pressure is relieved and people get burned.

But Barnabas is not out to burn. Not me or any pastor. His aim is healing. "That is part of why I wrote this book," he says, "to help PKs make sense of, sort through, and express those bottled-up frustrations and pains." Frustrations built up from carrying an "anvil-like weight," of being the most "watched"—"the best known and the least known people in the church."

But the boiling over does burn. "I have been hard on pastors throughout this book. I have pointed out weaknesses and tendencies and failures. I have prodded and demanded and pushed them to be different, to change, to become aware." My suggestion for the reader is that, if it gets too hot in the boiler room, you take a break from the heat, and jump in the pool of chapter eight.

There is a stream of grace that runs through this book. You taste it along the way. But it becomes a pool at the end. A soothing. Barnabas is honest about his own struggles and failures. He has drunk deeply at the fountain of grace. He knows from experience the ultimate solution for all of us:

> I desire to point to Jesus as the turner of hearts and the lifter of all burdens.... Grace, the undeserved favor of God, through Jesus, is the source of life and personhood and identity.... It is in the freedom of Jesus's overwhelming love that the PK can break out of false expectations and see what it is that makes Jesus happy.

As it turns out, when the boiling is over, and the burns begin to heal, there is hope for PKs and pastors and churches. "It's not all bad news for PKs." Through it all they have been unwitting, and sometimes unwilling, apprentices. They have seen—and many have benefited from—the bad and the good.

> We have seen the pleasures of ministry.... Helping mend a broken marriage, praying with a heartbroken widow, serving the destitute man who knocks at the door ... the close fellowship of a united church staff or ... the deep, humbling satisfaction of seeing God use faithful ministry over time to right a sinking ship of a church.

Boiling over because of painful experiences may be unavoidable at some point, but Barnabas beckons his fellow PKs not to "wallow and bemoan them. Rather we must own what responsibilities are ours: to honor Jesus, to honor our fathers and mothers, to love and support the church, and to go about our lives not as victims but as the redeemed. Grace is here for all of us."

And that includes the sinful and wounded pastors. "No man is adequate to be a pastor ... That is a job no person is up for, not alone, not without profound grace. And that is the key to all this: grace." And, of course, it is true for the wife and mother, watching, with tears, the drama play out between her son and husband, or bearing the weight of her daughter's rejection.

And finally there is grace for the church. "The church is our family, it's the family that God gave us, so don't give up on it. There isn't a better place out there to be restored."

When I received the manuscript of this book and read it, I gave a copy to our seventeen-year-old daughter. "Would you read this, and then talk to me about how I can be a better dad?" She did. It was a good talk. It's not over. I suspect she will have ideas about that when she is thirty and I am eighty. I hope she will be spared some sorrows because of her big brother's book. Of course, most of that hangs on me. And, as we have seen, on grace. Which is why I appreciated Barnabas's encouraging conclusion:

> But now I want to express thanks. I want to say that PKs are blessed to have parents who devote their lives to serving Jesus.... So thank you, pastors (and spouses). You have given your lives to serving Jesus and His church, and that is a blessing."
>
> John Piper

INTRODUCTION

March 31, 2013, Easter Sunday, was John Piper's last as the pastor of Bethlehem Baptist Church in Minneapolis, Minnesota. He was the senior pastor there for nearly thirty-three years. During his time as pastor, the church had grown from a few hundred to a few thousand people. They went from a traditional Baptist church in a rickety old building on the east side of downtown to a multicampus megachurch spread across the Twin Cities area. It was a long and fruitful tenure by both numeric measurements and those more significant ones—souls changed, hearts drawn to Jesus, and a passion for the supremacy of God spread.

John Piper is my father.

March 31, 2013, was also my thirtieth birthday. If you're quick with math, you'll realize that means the entirety of my life up to that day had been spent as a pastor's kid—a "PK." It was all I had known. I moved away from Minnesota for college when I was eighteen years old. Over the next decade I got married, had two children, and moved to the Chicago area. But all that change and progress does not remove me from the reality of being a PK. Once a PK, always a PK. It is an indelible mark.

Every child faces challenges in his or her upbringing. Every family suffers from idiosyncrasies, oddities, and faults. Everyone is a sinner brought up by sinners, so our stories all include foibles and face-plants before God and man alike. But I have found that there is uniqueness to the challenges PKs face. The reality of being a sinner on display in a ministry family creates quite the spiritual and emotional Molotov cocktail. And so I write this book, not as some sort of exposé on the miserable lives we PKs lead or about my family in particular, but to describe the unique challenges PKs have faced being the children of ministers.

The life of a PK is complex, occasionally messy, often frustrating, and sometimes downright maddening. It can be a curse and a bane. But being a PK can also be a profound blessing and provide wonderful grounding for a godly life. Often the greatest challenges are the greatest grounding and the biggest falls are the best blessings. This polarity exemplifies the challenge it is to be a PK.

For PKs, Pastors, and Congregants

My aim in writing this book is threefold. First, I want to speak for PKs, not as an expert observer or master researcher, but as one of them. I want to speak with honesty, humility, and clarity on behalf of those who face these unique challenges and don't know what to say to describe their struggles or how to say it. I want to give voice to the PK who doesn't know what to do with his challenges.

Second, I want to speak to pastors. Ministers of the gospel, your children are in an enormously challenging position. You are in an equally challenging position. While the prudent among you know this, I fear you may not fully understand the depths of the struggle they face (or will face). This is not a book to point an accusatory finger at the failures of pastors, although some will be dealt with, but to assist you in avoiding and remedying those failures. For some pastors this will be a harsh wake-up call, a bucket of ice water in your sleeping face. And that's good. If you're sleeping, you need it.

Third, I write to the church, because the congregation has more responsibility than it knows to care for and ease the burden of the pastor and his family. Too often the church has fostered a culture that puts enormous pressure on the pastor and his family. And by "the church" I don't mean just the organization, although that is included. I mean the collection of people who make up the church. It is people, individually, who contribute to the burden PKs carry, and I hope this book opens some eyes to things that need to change.

So as you forge ahead, know my heart in this book. I desire to see the hearts of fathers turned to their children and children to their fathers (and mothers, but being a good PK, I had to use the biblical phrasing). I long for burdens to be lifted and cast off, ones that have been carried since childhood. And I desire to point to Jesus as the turner of hearts and the lifter of all burdens.

What This Book Is Not

A final word about what you will find in these pages: one of the worst things that can happen in the relationship between reader and book is for there to be misconceptions or faulty expectations. So let me be clear on what this book is and is not.

I am not George Barna or Dave Kinnaman. Research and statistics are not my forte, so what you are about to read is not extrapolations and conclusions based on surveys and numerical data. Neither, though, is it a memoir or some sort of tell-all exposé of the dirty secrets of my family. This is not an autobiography telling the story of my upbringing. I don't think that would be interesting. Also, to write a memoir well, one has to be an artistic genius.

Instead, this is the conglomeration of dozens upon dozens of conversations I have shared with fellow PKs. It is drawn from emails and stories they have sent me. It is the result of a lifetime of observing my own family and the families of numerous other pastors I have had the chance to know. It is drawn from my own experience and the experiences of those close to me. Rather than tell a series of vignettes, I have woven these hundreds of experiences into a single person— the "PK." This means that I will share the story of the PK in broad, sweeping strokes. Not every PK will share all these experiences, but every PK will know of them.

I am not a church-health or pastoral-ministry expert either, so I will not offer a series of lessons or prescriptive chapters. I *am* an expert at being a PK (I can't really help that), so what you will find in these pages is the perspective of the PK shared in such a way as to help the church, the pastor, and my fellow PKs. My aim is to raise awareness of the struggles of PKs and give voice to a group of people who are often well recognized but little known.

When unpacking one's problems and struggles, it is easy to delve into psychology, developmental issues, family of origin, nature versus nurture, and the like. I am not qualified to do this either. Every PK has a different genetic makeup and a different environment in which they were brought up. Some are from tiny churches, and some from huge. Some moved around all the time, while others were at the same church for their entire childhood. Some are from distinctly conservative contexts, and others are from more liberal ones. All of this matters in the makeup of a PK. But I am not one to sort it out and explain it all. Instead, this will be a book of description, observation, and conglomeration.

Lastly, my intent in this book is not to hurt anyone, but hurt may happen. Pastors may feel attacked. Churches may feel criticized. PKs may feel exposed or even misrepresented. Please know this: I respect those in pastoral ministry, I am devoted to Christ's church, and as a PK, all I want to do is be a voice to bring about healthy change.

We will start at the beginning, by baring the soul of the PK. As we do this, other things will be exposed too, including some deficiencies of the church and its leaders. We will spend ample time on these but not in a melancholy, introspective way. Rather, we will be looking for the hope and restoration PKs need. It is there to be found.

Chapter 1

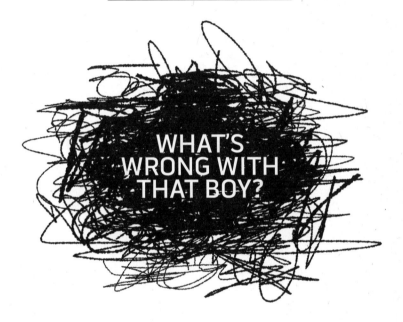

WHAT'S
WRONG WITH
THAT BOY?

"Oh, so you're a *PK*!" It's a punch line to a joke that doesn't even have to be told. That joke is my life, the life of a pastor's kid. PKs have a reputation. We are notorious troublemakers, rebels, rabble-rousers, and general miscreants. You can even tell we have a reputation because we get our own abbreviation. You don't see a teacher's kid getting called a "TK" or a salesman's kid getting called an "SK." This reputation is justly earned in many cases and goes back a long way. (For example, Captain Kidd, notorious seventeenth-century pirate and Presbyterian minister's son.)

Just as common as the outright troublemaker, though, is the PK who cares nothing for the faith of his father, who exits the church either in a slow drift or a dead sprint with his middle finger flying high. Other PKs might never leave the church, but their staying is rote and habitual rather than committed and passionate. Much has been written about church kids leaving the church and the faith,[1] but these are *pastors'* kids. They're supposed to be the good ones, the ones who know all the answers, the Bible quiz champions.

> "There are expectations that not only are pastors above sin and live holy lives but their children should as well."
>
> —Gail Hanson, PK

"They want the PK to dress like a grandparent and
behave like Jesus. But they also seem to wait for the
time when the pastor's daughter makes out and the
son drinks beer."

—Jeremy Noel, PK

Do you see the problem developing? Two paragraphs into this
chapter and we already have two conflicting stereotypes: the derisive
expectation of failure and the legalistic one of perfection. It's not
exactly an ideal choice for PKs to make because there is no right
answer. Walking away from the faith ends in destruction, while legalistic pursuit of perfection, well, it does too. In the end it feels as if
all we're left with is an uncomfortable position between a rock and a
hard place. Or we can just leave altogether.

Normal Kids, Abnormal Life

At our hearts, PKs are as normal as people get. We are born with a
variety of gifts, inclinations, propensities, and talents just like all the
other kids. Some of us love sports, some love to read, and others love
the arts. Some are quiet, and some are boisterous. Some of us are
lazy, and others are studious. Just like all the other kids. And just like
them we all have one thing in common: we're sinners. Every PK is
born from the same seed of Adam like every plumber's, banker's, or
musician's kid. It's important to state this up front because it is a step
toward setting the right expectations: sinners sin.

No, PKs aren't born different. There isn't some peculiar pastoral
DNA we've inherited that messes with our heads and hearts and

inclines us to a place of struggle. We're not born any more messed up than anyone else. Neither are we born less messed up as if some of the assumed pastoral sanctification has rubbed off on us. So why is it that all these PKs, the ones who seemingly have every biblical advantage, struggle to embrace and live in the faith of our fathers?

Let me answer that question with another question: Why do pastors go into ministry? I mean the good ones, the ones who love the Bible, have a passion for Jesus, and want to see people come to know Him. What is it that moves them to pursue the life of a pastor, to leave behind the hope of another career to become a shepherd of a wayward and wily flock? It is a calling, that inescapable pull on the heart and mind that draws him into the pastorate. And it is God who calls, so he follows. He has no other choice and no other desire.

And their spouses? When God calls, they respond too. The wife of a pastor is just as called to the ministry as the pastor himself and in many circumstances she bears the greater burden. She willingly joins her husband on this mission and sees her place in it. They live this life of ministry hand in hand and going in the same direction. His calling is her calling. (Yes, I know there are numerous instances of pastors dragging their spouses into the ministry. That is a separate problem altogether. I am describing those couples who desire to serve the Lord together.)

But what about their children? Are they old enough to be consulted? Not if they're unborn. Do they have any idea what Dad and Mom are setting out to do and be? Do they have any clue what this will mean for their lives? Even those kids who are old enough to sign off on the new job for Dad have no idea what this will mean for their lives. And those who have yet to be born are hosed. Dad and Mom might be following God's call, but these kids are just following Dad and Mom. What choice do they have?

A child doesn't know the call of his pastor father. All he knows is the effects it has on his life. He doesn't feel moved to ministry, because he's not. Yes, it is the call of the child to honor his parents, but that is not the same as a call to vocational ministry. The call of the father is not the call of the child, but the ministry of the father creates an anvil-like weight on the child. He just feels the pressure of it. Even the best pastoral parents can't protect their kids from this. And it is this pressure, in part, that drives so many PKs to break.

The Pressure Cooker

Cooking with a pressure cooker looks exactly like boiling food. It involves a big metal pot with water in it and a stove burner underneath. But it cooks food much faster than standard boiling does. Why is that? Because when water turns into steam and is trapped, it becomes pressurized and the pressurized steam reaches a much higher temperature. So instead of your food cooking at 212 degrees (water's boiling point), it cooks at close to 250 degrees. Not only that, though, the higher temperature and pressure create chemical reactions that can increase the rate of cooking by up to four times.

Why am I telling you this? Because being a PK can be very much like living in a pressure cooker. Even though we look just like the other kids and the ingredients are the same, our atmosphere is subtly but massively different. The ministry creates a pressure of expectation that is unlike any other. If all the other kids are cooking at 212 degrees (rather a challenge all its own), we are cooking at a scalding

250 pressurized degrees, and we are reaching our "done" point that much faster.

> "I certainly felt the pressure to be perfect."
> —Chriselda Dirrim, PK

The pastoral ministry isn't like other high-profile upbringings. It isn't like politics or Hollywood celebrity. Those both come with their pressures, certainly. But they don't come with the same unattainable expectations that so many PKs feel. A senator's child simply needs to look holy enough to not raise eyebrows; then she can escape the public eye. From there all she has to do is not get caught doing anything too stupid. For a PK, there is no choice but to *be* holy lest the name of Jesus and position of Daddy be shamed. The job itself requires holiness. Is it getting warm in here, or is it just me?

The Realities

Thus far all I have done is recognize the presence of challenges in the PK's life and given some vague allusions as to what they are. As we forge ahead through these chapters, we will explore the realities PKs face. But before we get going, I want to make clear the premise within which I work: PKs face unique obstacles that create an environment that can lead to significant spiritual, identity, and lifestyle challenges. Sometimes these are expressed as outright rebellion, and other times you might barely know they are there because the PK has so mastered the churchy arts as to slip his hypocrisy past the most astute deacon and Sunday school teacher.

Sometimes these struggles are so embedded in the souls of PKs that they don't even know if they really believe what they grew up believing. Sometimes they can't diagnose the struggles at all and have no idea they even exist. For me, it wasn't until I hit a massive spiritual crisis in my midtwenties that I began to recognize the depths of my spiritual identity issues. I was broken first by the weight of sin, then by the weight of grace. Sins that had festered in my heart for decades were exposed and ripped out. It hurt like a little sliver of hell. My false identity that hid so much dishonesty and nastiness was crushed by God's gracious discipline, and I was left with … what? What was I?

In the healing and restoring since then, I have seen that much of who I thought I was prior to that came from my father's teaching and the force of his ministry; but it was not my own. I did not own it or feel comfortable in it. And it did not own me or comfort me. I was lost even though I knew every inch of the map. In short, John Piper's Jesus was not Barnabas Piper's. Barnabas Piper did not know the real Jesus.

This is not to say I was not saved. It is to say I did not have a relationship with Jesus that was deep, close, personal, and truly life-changing. By God's grace I have not rejected that teaching or the faith my dad tried to instill in me during my growing-up years. Neither, though, have I followed neatly in his footsteps. I have my own opinions, my own thought processes, my own convictions. I am developing as a man and as a follower of Jesus differently than he did. I have different gifts, hobbies, and convictions about many things. The faith, the reality of Jesus Christ as my only hope, though, is one I share with my father. But it took utter breaking at the hand of God over sin in my life to get me there. It was not my identity as a PK that saved me. It was grace.

And so it is for all PKs who follow Jesus. As I have spoken with pastors' kids from around the country, I have been amazed by how many have fallen away from Jesus. But I am also amazed by how many live their lives for Him with passion and purpose. Both outcomes seem so unlikely, and sometimes they are the same PKs who do both—walk away and then live for Jesus. And so, as we move forward, know that this isn't a book of hopelessness or doomsday soothsaying. God's grace is bigger than these struggles. This is a glimpse into the realities PKs live as they are pressure-cooked in the ministry of their parents.

Our stories are different. Our parents are different. Our churches are different. But the pressures are largely the same. Our struggles are the same. And so we set off to know those struggles, to seek ways to avoid them, and to find what God would have us learn from them.

Chapter 2

THE FISHBOWL

"I can remember my mother telling me at a very young age that we were always being watched. That still stays with me until today."

—Jordan Taylor, PK

"Being a pastor's kid puts the kind of spotlight on a family, and subsequently the children, that can cause difficulties."

—Tyler Braun, PK

"Everyone's eyes are on you. All the time."

—Valor Poland, PK

On a purely lifestyle level, one of the greatest challenges PKs face is scrutiny. It feels perpetual and persistent, even invasive. PKs are like everyone else in that we want to be *known*; we want people to know our hearts and our fears and what makes us us. But this sort of scrutiny creates a horde of people who know volumes *about* us. It creates a tension in which it can be difficult to genuinely make ourselves known, and so PKs become both the best-known and the least-known people in the church. In most cases there isn't a single person or a particular group of people doing the watching. It's a collective, disorganized, largely unintentional effort on the part of the church as a whole. At best it is bothersome; at worst it is suffocating and warping.

This sort of pervasive scrutiny is not an obvious thing. It is not composed of people snooping or spying or skulking. The primary result of scrutiny is awareness, or maybe what one might call "hyper-awareness." People simply become constantly aware of the PK in ways that differ from their awareness of other kids. This is a subtle problem because people don't even realize their heightened awareness. Folks in the church just glean things about the PK's life from sermon illustrations (and pastors wonder why kids hate being used in sermons) or from a conversation here and a passing comment there. This is information that wouldn't even register or come up at all if it wasn't about the pastor's kid. It is all innocent in motive and accidental in action.

My dad has a sermon called "Doing Missions When Dying Is Gain."[2] It is one that has become sort of a seminal message for his ministry. The thing that stands out to me about it, though, is one little story, the story of me as a little boy running home crying after a group of boys in our inner-city neighborhood had stolen my bike. As the story goes, my dad saw this as an opportunity to teach me about suffering and making sacrifices for the gospel. And that is what the story means to the thousands of people who have heard that message now. You know what it meant to me? It meant hurt, embarrassment, and sadness at the loss of a bike, the kind of sadness only a little boy can have at the loss of his favorite toy. In the years since that message became popular, at least a dozen people, mostly strangers, have asked me about that story—a story that in any normal circumstance they wouldn't even know. They know something about me. They have gained an awareness of me. These strangers shouldn't even know my name, yet now they have questions about a private moment from my childhood.

The pressure of this sort of expansive awareness builds on the shoulders of the PK through small things, the side comments people make about things they have no business knowing. These comments aren't usually malicious, just misplaced. People feel they "know" the PK, so they ask about his football game last Saturday. That's really nice, but how do they even know about that? Or a woman might congratulate him for getting into a particular college. Thanks, ma'am. Who are you again?

Every one of these little comments expresses an awareness of the details of life. A PK might hear ten comments or questions on a Sunday from ten different people, each of whom has no intention whatsoever of prodding or snooping. Even the sheer number of people who greet the PK by name is constricting. It all adds up to a feeling of being watched. And watched is what PKs so often do feel, all the time, in everything. It is life in a fishbowl, exposed, on display.

Well-Known but Unknown

People love to be known. We are relational beings whether we express it as vivacious extroversion or conversational introversion. Being known is safe, secure, warm. It has been in our DNA since the very beginning when Adam walked with God and Eve was created to be *with* Adam as a mate and helper. He needed her companionship because he was designed to need it. Even Jesus, the Trinitarian Son of God who has been eternally in relationship, surrounded Himself with twelve close friends, three of them His very closest. Being known is freeing because it means we can be ourselves with all our flaws, quirks, doubts, fears, paradoxes, and secrets. It is something that isn't easily found and ought to be fiercely protected and fostered. A significant problem arises though, when we confuse being *known of* for being known.

Being *known of* is intoxicating. It is exciting to be recognized by relative strangers. It gives a sense of influence (real or imagined) and even power. It makes one feel special. This is why people are so willing to do idiotic things to get "famous." Reality TV is full of people selling their dignity so they will be *known of.* Being known of is also the state that PKs find themselves in, albeit hopefully in a different context than contestants on *Big Brother.*

Being so well-known in the church circle has its advantages. It can feel good to be popular. It can open doors to certain opportunities, and it provides a feeling of being liked. Who doesn't want to be liked? But there is a flip side to being known in this way.

The more people know about a person, the more they think they know him. That is to say the more they assume about him. As a PK, it can be tremendously difficult to get from known of to known because of these assumptions.

The Assumptions of Awareness

Very few people in the church would vocalize their assumptions about the PK or even cognitively recognize that they hold them, but they are present. For example, some people assume all is well, that the PK has it all together. They're usually wrong; remember, PKs are as human as everyone else. Others are intimidated by the PK: he must know more Bible verses, be wiser, and have a secure line to God's office in heaven. Nope, not usually. And then there's the family assumption: the PK has a *pastor* for a dad, and his mom leads the women's, children's, hospitality, shut-in, quilt-making, and baking ministries, so what could a normal old congregant offer him? False assumption. The normal congregant can offer something powerful to a PK, usually many things.

PKs want to be known, not just known of. We want to be in relationships that cut through the facades and fronts and unearth the insecurities and needs. We long for those friends and mentors who will willfully set aside all they think they know of us as PKs and get to know us as people. These friends will engage our passions, our interests, our fears, our confusions. Throughout my life since high school, I have had these friends. They are the ones who will call me out on a lie or grapple with sins alongside me or forgive when I sin against them. They pay no mind whatsoever to who my father is and instead look straight into my life and see me. They are the ones who have been there for my worst days and helped me come through them. They *know* me. PKs struggle, and if all we have are people around us who know of us, we bottle those struggles inside and the pressure builds. Being known is a release, a way to pour out our problems and be helped, supported, corrected, taught, and simply *known*.

> "Early on in my life I was viewed as 'the good kid' by so many outside of our family that pride and self-reliance were watered in my heart."
>
> —Ryan Davidson, PK

"I think they just assumed that since I always behaved and had the right answer, I was okay."

—Valor Poland, PK

"Where is there a safe place to go with your struggles? Who can you talk to? Not even the pastor…"

—Valor Poland, PK

People make many other assumptions about PKs. Here are five of the most pervasive. There are others and variations of these, but these five run amok in churches.

The PK Has a Great Relationship with God

PKs are sinners. We laid that out pretty clearly up front. This means that, just as for everyone else, our connection to God is broken without Jesus. We don't gain relationship with God by osmosis from our dads, regardless of their scriptural studies or dynamic preaching. Our moms' faithful service can't do a thing to wash away our sins. No, we need to get to know Jesus and be won by Him. I will dig deeper into why this is such a challenge for PKs later on, but for now just know that this is a bogus assumption. A PK's relationship with God may or may not be healthy, but the fact that his dad is a pastor plays no role in determining that.

The PK Has a Great Relationship with His Family

The reality that PKs are normal humans (as much as anyone is "normal") is the drumbeat of this book in some ways. I keep bringing it up because so much of the expectation and assumption for us is abnormal. Like this assumption, for example: Take a healthy family with a hardworking set of parents who love their children, children who study hard and play hard and obey hard. Think about how much conflict that family has on a daily basis about whose turn it is to sit in the front seat, who's supposed to take out the trash, or why Dad missed Junior's soccer game. Then realize that healthy families aren't the norm. Add the pressures of an entire church of dysfunctional people to that family, throw in odd hours, tight finances (in many pastors' families), and all the awareness and assumptions addressed thus far. Exactly how healthy can a PK's relationship with his family be expected to be?

God's grace is very big, and there are numerous ministry families that are healthy. But this cannot be assumed. Ministry is a burden on families, one that is worth bearing for many, but a burden nonetheless. To assume that PKs have great relationships with their parents and siblings is to make dangerous assumptions about all parties involved. Dad is a sinner, Mom is a sinner, siblings are sinners. Only by grace can relationships between those people add up to healthy.

The PK Loves the Church

PKs have a complicated relationship with the church. Many love it and are devoted to it just as their parents are. Many depend on it for their identities and to reinforce who they are. It is a safe place where they are confident and well liked. I spoke with one PK who described how difficult it was to transition from church and Christian school life to public school life when her family moved from one town to another. One culture was safe and sheltered for her. The other was overwhelming and terrifying. Church was her haven and identity, for better and worse.

Many PKs resent church as a place of high expectations and hypocrisy. For others, it is the place of business for their fathers. For me, it was some combination of the above. But my relationship with the church was never pure, unadulterated love. I did love it, and at times I hated it too. I hated the pressure and the expectations. I resented that it was the entity around which my family orbited. To assume that a PK loves the church is to oversimplify what is a tricky relationship.

The PK Is Confident in His Beliefs

Often the church is not a safe place to have doubts, or at least it doesn't feel safe. And during a child's growing up, he will reach a point where it isn't cool to not know something either, so confidence is the front he puts up. On top of that is the expectation that PKs so often feel to be a biblical scholar extraordinaire. I remember the pressure to get the right answer to nail every Sunday school question.

One instance is burned into my mind. My second-grade class was playing a trivia game, and the teacher threw out the question "Which prophet in the Bible was known as 'the grieving prophet'?" I would bet good money the teacher wouldn't have even known that one if he hadn't been holding the answer key. There was total silence. Nobody knew this one. So after a few moments of children squirming, the teacher locked eyes with me and said, "Barnabas, you want to give it a guess?" No, of course I didn't. I had a reputation to uphold. But this was a challenge; a line had been drawn in the sand,

and I had been triple dog dared like Flick in *A Christmas Story*.[3] I had no choice. I racked my brain for all the prophets I could think of and eventually croaked out, "Jeremiah?" *Yes!* Right answer. And of course getting that one right is one reason I remember this story so clearly. The other reason is because I had been called out individually like that. But why had I been singled out to answer? I'm thinking the answer lies somewhere in the letters *PK*.

But there is a huge difference between knowledge of biblical facts and confidence in biblical reality. For some PKs, doubts and questions arise about even the very existence of God, the foundation of all faith. For others, and maybe more commonly, it's questions like "Is obeying God's Word really going to make me happier than following my emotions?" The biblical realities of grace, forgiveness, and identity in Christ can seem unreal and unattainable to PKs no matter how steeped in the Bible we have been since we could walk and talk. And, in fact, being so steeped in all things biblical often makes those realities harder to believe because they seem mundane, even though they are the basis for all good things. Do not assume that PKs are confident in their beliefs. Often we do not even know what we believe even if we can spout off every biblical reference about that which we know we should believe.

> "I think the greatest challenge of being a PK is developing a personal relationship with God/Jesus, etc. By this I mean it can be easy to assume that the faith of our fathers will blanket our lives and we can just ride their coattails."
>
> —Jon Stepan, PK

The PK Is a Leader

Like father, like son, right? Dad leads the church; I lead the youth group. Mom leads the women's ministry; I lead a small group. It is so easy to look at the progeny of the pastor and assume they are ready to slide into roles of leadership. And if a PK is anything like me, he will feel a sort of right to those roles; he will adopt the expectation as reality. And we would both be wrong. It is foolish for you to assume I am ready to lead and more foolish for me to assume I deserve to do so.

Leadership ought to be an earned role. A PK may or may not earn it, but simply being the PK is not qualification enough. This is typical of Americans, though. So often we assume a person has leadership qualities because of the family name or the good looks or the booming voice. We assume qualifications based on associations. PK is just another of those hollow qualifiers for leadership; it means nothing. Being a PK is to leadership what an Armani power suit is to being a good lawyer. It just fools people into thinking we fit the bill.

There is something to be said for genetics and upbringing. If Dad and Mom have qualities of leadership and have raised their kids well, then it's more likely that the PKs will be ready to lead. But even then we should be vetted for the right attitudes (something I so often lack), the right morals, the right reputation just like any other potential leadership candidate. Nothing in being a PK inherently makes us leaders.

What is more, many PKs want nothing to do with leadership. Maybe they are shy. Maybe they lack confidence. Maybe they are content to absorb and participate but want nothing to do with being up-front. And this is okay! Leadership is not for everyone. Pushing the PK into leadership based on a faulty assumption hurts both the unready or unwilling leader and those who are supposed to follow him.

From Awareness to Assumptions to Expectations

Think of your favorite athlete or actor or author. As you follow their respective careers, you develop an awareness of them, their work, and often their personal lives. Subconsciously you form opinions and assumptions about them as people, and as these assumptions form, they turn into expectations. It's a natural progression. When I was in elementary school, Kirby Puckett of the Minnesota Twins was my favorite athlete. I owned dozens of his baseball cards (still do, in fact), memorized his stats, loved watching him play baseball, and generally revered him. I never consciously thought about Kirby as a man, mostly just as a baseball player. However, because I loved the man in uniform who played baseball so well, I began to subconsciously assume certain things about him as a person. So when I found out Kirby was charged with sexually assaulting a woman at a restaurant, I was stunned. Over time, it came out that Kirby was not the cherubic figure I had envisioned. He had a lengthy list of indiscretions, and I had projected my favorable opinion of a ballplayer onto him as a man. I had formed baseless expectations and set myself up for disappointment.

While most PKs aren't famous and don't claim to be, the principle applies. The awareness of them leads to assumptions, like the ones addressed above, and then to expectations. We'll look at these expectations, so often baseless and oppressive, in the next chapter. They are powerful and often harmful forces in the lives of PKs.

Chapter 3

EXPECTATION
ROLLER
COASTER

"Some people in the church expect PKs to be mini versions of their parents."

—Adam Engebretson, PK

I was seventeen years old and rolling in my parents' blue 1991 Chevy Lumina and pushing the factory-made stereo to its tinny max with Linkin Park's *Hybrid Theory*. Windows down, seat reclined, I cruised into the church parking lot closely behind two friends in their cars blaring tunes equally as loud, each of us competing for the title of "most obnoxious punk listening to music he will later realize is rubbish." Boys will be boys, right?

Wrong. Not this boy. As soon as I sauntered into the church, I was pulled aside and roundly chastised for my choice of both band and decibel level. Those friends likely don't recall this incident at all. That's because they weren't chastised at all. They were just boys being boys, while I was the PK being an idiot.

Legalism Crystalized

Legalism creates false expectations. It is a false standard of holiness based on some extrabiblical standard, some man-made understanding of morality. And just like any false expectation, the inevitable result is disappointment. In the instance I just described, I was the victim of a false expectation—the PK will not act in such a manner—and was thus the cause of disappointment that led to angst. But the problem was not just the particularity of the expectation, it was the inconsistency. Or rather the hypocrisy of the double standard. Two boys did something and walked away unchastised. The PK did the same and got dressed down. The woman didn't have a problem with the music, just that I was the one who was listening to it. Or maybe she felt that, as the PK, I was public property to be corrected as she saw fit, while my friends were someone else's problem.

Legalism creates more than just an inability to reach the moral standard. It creates an inability to even figure out what that standard is because it breeds hypocrisy. It points at other people's sins while ignoring one's own, and it creates standards of holiness that apply only to some. While this is rampant throughout the church, nowhere is it as clear as in the life of a PK. What is true for churchgoers the world over in a subdued way is unveiled in all its dastardly glory when it comes to PKs—a double standard selected outside of a clear understanding and expression of grace. Or maybe it's a triple or quadruple standard. The truth is I never could figure it out.

The legalism and hypocrisy that the church can barely keep a lid on become crystalized in the PK's experiences. While the same woman who chewed me out for my music selection (Or was it the volume? Or maybe how fast I was driving? Or the squeal of the tires?) may have quietly looked askance at my friends, she felt free to light me up like a Christmas tree. This is a lighthearted example of a PK's experience of hypocritical expectations. Other examples are not always so easy to shrug off, especially when they happen day after day from person after person for any number of reasons. These false expectations can crush a soul. And there are many.

> "I heard constantly, 'You're a preacher's kid! Preachers' kids shouldn't say/do that,' and I *hated* it. I didn't so much hate being held to a standard of behaving well, but my standard was much, much higher than anyone else's merely because my father was a pastor."
>
> —Jeremy Lloyd, PK

The Perfect Angel

Probably the easiest false expectation to pinpoint is that of godly behavior, or rather the sort of behavior traditional Christianity has labeled as "godly." The story I started this chapter with is a perfect example. I was held to a different standard than my peers. And there are numerous stories like that one, but they can be summed up easily in a single phrase: "You can't do that; you're a pastor's kid!" Whether it is cussing on the basketball court, playing pranks on Sunday school teachers, fighting in the youth room, playing music too loud, going to R-rated movies (or any movie, for that matter), yelling at siblings, mouthing off to parents, or any number of other very normal childhood actions, that sentiment presides over all for numerous PKs.

One PK I know told me a story of going home from college for a holiday break. Some friends asked him to join them at a pool hall to play a few games of eight ball. Being under the legal drinking age, he wisely decided to abstain from the beer that his older friends enjoyed. They shot some pool, had a good time, and headed home. Two days later a church member called his father to report having seen him at the bar and to express concern about his behavior. Thankfully, in this case, his parents already knew of his time out and were fine with it. The greater point is the expectation that he "ought not to have been in such a place," not to mention the eagle eye it took to spot him there. Would this church member have made the same call if it was any other college kid from church? Maybe (in which case he was just a narc), but probably not. The church member had a singular expectation of the PK.

There is a straightforward, blunt, in-your-face expectation that PKs will behave "better" than our peers. We will have inherently better judgment, avoid temptations common to our age and gender, express none of our baser thoughts or feelings, and generally reflect positively on our parents and their position. Which is total nonsense. (Especially when you consider the reputation PKs have for being rebels and deviants. Wait, am I supposed to be an angel or a devil? Now I'm all confused.)

This expectation is, most often, piled on from the outside. People in the church react with surprise at normal childhood behavior. But it is not at all uncommon for pastors themselves to hold their children to a higher moral standard. Such a standard can be expressed terribly, something like "When you act like that, Son, it reflects poorly on me as a pastor." Or it can be couched in more biblical terms and expressed as a standard of "honoring God" and "representing Jesus" well. Either way though, PKs face a standard that we *know* is not the same as everyone else's.

"I would be frequently trotted out as a moral example to others."

—Jonathan Holmes, PK

This kind of multiple standard causes PKs to focus on the wrong things. We begin to worry about pleasing people. Or we begin to resent them. It runs the risk of casting God in the same light as the crotchety old woman who's always griping about our baggy pants, shaggy hair, and thumping bass. It really doesn't matter if the double standard is unintended and the desire is truly to raise kids who honor God with their actions. PKs are so often getting it from all sides that even the well-meaning pastor-parent needs to realize that what is needed most is extreme grace and powerful expressions of love while deemphasizing the significance of behavior as the gold standard. Behavior does matter. Obedience to God and parents matters, but this kind of grace counteracts the pressure to be defined by behavior that PKs so often feel. We need an extra measure of grace to overcome the lack of grace we find in so many areas of life.

All-Star Bible Scholar

Beyond being well-mannered, all-star kids, PKs aren't allowed to not know the Bible. Even dating back to my earliest Sunday school memories, I was expected to be the Bible answer guy. I remember playing Bible Baseball, a game in which the class of peewees was divided into two teams and would set a "lineup," the order in which we would answer Bible trivia questions. The teacher would begin posing questions to the team who was "at bat" first, and the "hitter" (answerer) would choose whether he wanted to go for a single, double, triple, or home run, each of which was a question of increasing difficulty. Of course this all sounds like a quirky, fun way to imprint some Bible facts onto impressionable minds. But it wasn't all that innocent.

I felt the pressure to be more than just a "hitter." I had to be a slugger, to swing for the trivial fences with every at bat. I was the pastor's son, and pastors' kids don't settle for base hits when there are home runs to be crushed. And it didn't stop there, because with every home run or triple, every correct answer (and there were many, if I do say so), the expectation of my biblical savvy became a self-fulfilling prophecy. In my own mind and the minds of my teachers and classmates I was a burgeoning biblical expert. At eight years old, the course was set, the identity determined. John Piper's son is a Bible answer man.

Numerous PKs face this expectation. A teacher or small group leader poses a question to a group of students, and after a moment of awkward silence, eyes begin to glance toward the PK as if to say, "Why don't you take this one." And so the PK is put in an unenviable position—fulfill the expectation, which will only lead to greater expectations later, or admit that she doesn't want to answer. Or maybe, God forbid, she doesn't know the answer. And over time, Sunday after Sunday, small group after small group, this tension can build into a muddled, confused identity.

Theologian Extraordinaire

In some sense the "Bible expert" identity is one that PKs can't help. It takes very intentional effort *not* to learn biblical facts and references when it is your parents' full-time job and home life both. We absorb biblical knowledge passively whether we care to or not. And the higher expectation naturally follows.

When you combine this ever-present reality with the fact that we are the progeny of clergy, a further challenge arises—PKs are often expected to be theologians (sometimes by our parents, usually by the church). This is distinctly different than being a "Bible expert," someone who knows the facts of Scripture. Being a theologian is a discipline, a cause, a passion. People expect that one of our great passions will be the systematized exploration and explanation of God. And while it is good for everyone to give careful thought to the things of God, the expectation of "theologian" placed on PKs is much more than that.

Pastors are called. To them, theology is the lifeblood of the job. Biblical scholars have devoted themselves to the study of the text and its nuances. If their motives are good, they do this out of deep excitement, curiosity, and a desire to understand and explain deeper realities. Pastors and scholars are uniquely gifted to such work. Just as accountants have skills and interest in numbers and athletes have skills and interest in sports, so pastors and scholars have skills and interest in theology. But that doesn't mean their kids do.

In spite of the obvious reality that PKs aren't all, or even mostly, interested in being theologians, the expectation still exists that we ought to be. When we are young, this expectation looks a lot like the Bible expert one: We are called upon to answer questions and looked to by our peers to step up when there is a prickly issue about God. As we grow older, parishioners want to discuss the finer points of the sermon or the latest controversial blogs or books.

Many PKs simply don't care that much about the finer points of theology, and in that way we are very much like most Christians. But we are not allowed to be normal Christians. The expectation is for us to be exceptional Christians.

Stay in Your Lane

These three expectations—perfect angel, biblical superstar, and theologian extraordinaire—are ingredients to a greater pressure that many PKs feel. Each of these three is a clear face of legalism, easy to discern. But a greater pressure comes about when they are added together. It is harder to put a finger on. It is the pressure to *believe*, to stay in the proper theological, denominational, or lifestyle lane.

My father is a right-lane, speed-limit driver. I am not. Whenever I need to follow him anywhere, it chafes. I don't even know how to drive fifty-five in the right lane; doing so makes me feel like I'm going in reverse. But if I know where I'm going, it's no big deal for me to move to the left lane, give him a wave, and buzz on ahead to meet him at the destination. I go at my own pace and get there in my time. But that's not the way it works as a PK in the rest of life. PKs are raised knowing exactly what we are supposed to believe. We know the theology of our parents, the moral framework of our family and church, the expressions of Christianity that are "right." We are expected to follow nicely in the convoy of our family and church, to maintain the speed limit and, under no circumstances, change lanes and go on ahead.

The Theological Lane

I was raised in a Baptist, Calvinistic,[4] complementarian[5] context. The Bible was the greatest authority and absolutely true. My father was a scholar of it, having received a master's degree from Fuller Theological Seminary as well as a doctorate in theology from the University of Munich. He has written dozens of books. Up until his retirement from the pastorate, he would spend dozens of hours each week in study, reading, and sermon preparation. A clear and bold understanding of theology was the filter through which all decisions were made. This held true in our church as well. It was a theologically rigorous place with an emphasis on biblical teaching and theological continuity.

For other PKs, the story is different. Maybe they were raised as fundamentalist dispensationalists, Pentecostals, or in the social gospel. Maybe they were in a King James–only context or a more attractional church environment that emphasized felt needs and welcoming outsiders. Whatever the context, though, the implicit understanding is that we will stay in that lane. We will believe the same things and express our beliefs the same way too.

The Denominational Lane

Admittedly, this expectation is far more significant for some PKs than others. But when it is an expectation, it is a *big* one. Denomination is identity for many. It is the safe place. A Baptist kid couldn't even consider becoming a Methodist or a Lutheran. A Lutheran better not consider Presbyterianism or the Evangelical Free Church. Those are where all the crazies are.

For me growing up, denomination wasn't really a thing, except that I just *knew* all the paedobaptists[6] were some combination of crazy and evil. When we went to the neighboring Lutheran church for joint holiday services, it felt like entering an alien spaceship where people wore robes and smelled funny. Denomination wasn't an identity in itself, but it was a tradition I was tied to. For many PKs, though, it is much more than that. To leave would be to betray a trust or to go over to the dark side.

The Lifestyle Lane

Just as each church has its theological distinctives, it also has a lifestyle culture, a moral framework. Maybe this is based on biblical interpretation, or maybe (more commonly) it is tradition. I am not referring to explicit biblical commands (don't steal, don't commit adultery or fornicate, don't be a drunk, etc.). I mean the boundaries our churches have for everything else.

We don't drink, we don't chew, and we don't go with girls who do. Alcohol is of the Devil. TV rots your brain. Dating is bad, so you should only court—or better yet, have an arranged marriage. Smoking will not only kill you, it will send you to hell. Tattoos are evil. Syncopated rhythm is the gateway for the Devil to enter your body and make you move in sensual ways. If Jesus comes back while you're watching an R-rated movie, He'll leave you behind. You know that bit George Carlin did about seven words you can't say on TV? Well, you can't say them here either. Nor can you say anything that hints of maybe meaning something a little bit like them. All food eaten before you pray will rot in your belly. A penny saved is a penny earned, and one out of every ten pennies better go to the church, or else. The church doors are open, so you better be there. And so on.

Of course these are the extremes. Many churches aren't like that, but there is still a lifestyle expectation. Each of us knows what it is, or was, at our church. We all know there is an "out of bounds." There is an understanding of how church views and relates to culture—enemies, tense neighbors, the strange unknown, the terrible threat, the object of pity, the target of love and affection. Going out of bounds is out of the question. To do so is to fail—fail our families, our churches, our God.

Pressure

To change lanes is not just to break with tradition. It is to betray. For many PKs, to go a different direction from our upbringing is hurtful to our parents. Pastors *own* their beliefs; their theology and public ministry make up an identity. So when their children refuse to follow, it is personal, not merely ideological. It is a rift in the relationship, not just a difference of opinion. This has been the case in my own family. My father does not preach ideas; to him, they are reality. Trying to separate him from his ministry and theology is impossible. As my brothers and I have gone in different directions at different times, the family has encountered tension. My father sees one way of connecting and relating to God. My brothers and I have seen others and pursued them. Working through such tensions can be painful.

I need to point out, though, that my analogy is of changing lanes, not taking different roads to different places. Numerous PKs decide to go entirely different directions than our parents. Maybe it is a rejection of God altogether or a choice of lifestyle that is completely counterbiblical. That isn't what I'm referring to here. I'm talking about the PK who is going to the same location as his parents, who wants to follow God. But he doesn't want to follow his parents' fifty-five miles per hour car in the right lane. He wants to go his own way but meet them there, at the place of honoring God. The problem is that many pastors see the mere changing of lanes as taking a detour to nowhere. It draws knee-jerk reactions, and is seen as a personal affront, even as an assault on the ministry.

The same is true to a different degree within the church. A PK is expected to be a chip off the old block, so to go a different direction is to draw fire. "What would your father think?" becomes a refrain. Everyone in the church knows the pastor's standards. They are proclaimed weekly from the pulpit. So now everyone gets to hold the PK to that standard.

For me, and other PKs whose parents have a large profile, this expands beyond the church itself. My father speaks nationally and internationally. His books have sold millions of copies and influenced many. His theology and views are well-known and have been adopted by tens of thousands. So what happens when I put up a blog post or write an article that differs from him? What happens when I post on Twitter about something he would take issue with? I get that same question—"What would your father think?"—from all corners. The pressure to stay in my lane comes from Facebook, Twitter, blog comments, and email.

What are PKs to do? How do we respond? The reality is, and I speak for numerous PKs, I do not care what my father thinks about many things. I am not a chip off the old block. He has influenced me and taught me, and now I am taking my own lane and going my own speed. And that is what PKs must be able to do. We must choose to do it, and the church must let us.

My Own Lane, Not My Own Road

I mentioned earlier that I'm not talking about the PK who wants to reject all things about God in response to false expectations. I'm talking about the one who wants to follow God in a way that fits her, not the way that fits her parents or her church tradition. I am talking about the PK who feels differently about certain aspects of Christianity than her parents and expresses her faith differently. It is not a different faith or a different God. It is a different expression and passion and person. We aren't our parents.

The expectations placed on PKs make this freedom of exploration and expression massively difficult. We feel guilt about doing things differently, even when we are doing good things. We feel guilt for thinking new thoughts, even when they are good thoughts. There is no room for challenging tradition, even when tradition is wrong. And there is absolutely, positively, no room for doubt.

The PK must represent Jesus, her family, and the church at all times. It matters not whether she truly knows who Jesus is. There isn't any time or room for figuring that out. Jesus is who we PKs were told He is. It doesn't matter if we agree with our family. Dad is the pastor, so buck up and be good. As a member of the church's figurehead family, you carry that banner with you wherever you go, so don't drop it.

Confusion

It is a perplexing mess of expectations for PKs, too much for many to navigate well. There is so little room for learning and figuring things out. Even those who come through healthy in mind and soul have stories to tell, and there are too many who don't come through happy and healthy. The constant pressure to *be* something, *do* something, and *believe* something creates enormous confusion for PKs. And one of the main confusions is about who we are, an identity crisis.

Chapter 4

IDENTITY
CRISIS

"Who am I?" is a question that's difficult for anyone to answer. So often it devolves into questions about our circumstances, and the most common one in America is "What do you do?" Our jobs or hobbies become our identities. I am a writer. I am a banker. I am a biker or a runner. And maybe those are the things some people actually see as the core of their being, the defining aspect of their personhood. But I think most people, even as they label themselves, know there is more to them than just that. They know their jobs and hobbies and families don't define them or give them an identity. If only they could figure out what does.

Think back over the expectations that we looked at for PKs. Consider the effect those have on our ability to determine our identity. We have been told since we were tiny, both implicitly and explicitly, what we are to be and how we are to be that thing. We have been told what to believe and how to believe it. There is little or no room for self-expression or exploration since we *know* the right way to do things. PKs are, more often than not, put in a box with a nice label on the outside and no breathing room on the inside. That is our identity to those around us. It's a bit suffocating.

> "It was like I was being separated and placed in a separate category."
>
> —Angela Jackson, PK

In order to handle expectations, to navigate them well, know-ing one's identity is essential. Expectations create pressure, and only a strong identity is able to withstand it. In a healthy situation a gradual increase in expectations occurs as a child grows so that, over time, he is able to learn who he is, who God is, and how to stand firm in the face of external pressure. For PKs, though, the expectations and the pressure create the identity; few of us have the shelter in which to grow and learn and become strong. The home of a spiritual shepherd should be a safe haven for children to find truth, but it is often as pressure packed as everywhere else or more so.

In response to this box, this external pressing to *be* something, PKs often struggle. Sometimes we make a willful decision to fight back. Most often, though, we instinctively respond to things not being as they should be, we reflexively react to the situation. Whether we consciously resist or simply react, one thing holds true: these struggles can be wickedly dangerous for a PK's soul because they lead to a false identity. The PK's identity becomes defined by trying to be something we are not or trying not to be something demanded of us. Either way, our identity doesn't have a healthy aim and a productive goal. We are aiming *away* from something, which leaves us without a definitive bull's-eye, a true target.

The Tricks of the Trade

In any role or job some essential skills are necessary for optimum success. They aren't taught, but they are learned. Often they aren't the "rules" or even proper techniques. They are those cracks in the listed skills and job description, the little white spaces that a person learns how to fill up to become maximally effective. They are the tricks of the trade. Just as salesmen learn to upsell with charm and stories and a good basketball player knows how to foul without getting caught, so too PKs learn tricks of their "trade." These are the subtle, often instinctive, and maybe even accidental methods and skills that allow PKs to survive and present the desired persona, to "be" whatever is expected or necessary.

The Onion

"Ogres are like onions." This succinct line from *Shrek*, the animated monster famously voiced by Mike Myers, sums up PKs too. Shrek goes on to explain, "Layers! Onions have layers; ogres have layers." My point is not to draw a comparison between PKs and ogres, much as that might fit in some cases. Still, what you see is not always what you get with PKs. What is on the outside is not all there is.

Few people can do hypocrisy more smoothly than a PK. On the outside he is devout, polite, and involved. On the inside he is cold, angry, and detached. Or maybe he is simply confused. Either way, he is not as he presents himself. He doesn't know what he is, but he knows what he is supposed to be, so that's the face you see.

> "I simply was the kid who was basically doing the least amount of visible evil, who knew most of the answers in the Sunday school class, and a sense of false humility grew in my heart."
>
> —Ryan Davidson, PK

To make matters more difficult, nobody knows all the right answers better than a PK. We even know the answers to the questions about our answers. With most kids you can dig a little, ask a few insightful questions, and bingo, you find the inconsistency or hypocrisy. Not so with PKs. PKs know the right answers, know the questions that are coming, know the answers to those questions, and thus can leave you with no true idea of their own heart's beliefs. If that's not bad enough, all these right answers leave the PK himself not knowing the difference between what he knows he should say and what he believes.

For fifteen years, this described me. I was the extroverted, confident, upstanding son of a famous preacher. I was well versed in the Bible, able to win most arguments with my peers, and quite sure of myself. I could be earnest, charismatic, serious, or lighthearted as the situation demanded. But what was on the outside was not what was on the inside. Inside I was confused. I had no direction in life. After college I got a job and did well, but I had little passion for it even though the company did excellent ministry, served the church well, and had leaders with character and integrity. Inside I was muddled, and much of that was because I was attached to certain sins. I was living a lie, and nobody—I mean *nobody*—knew it. Only God and I knew, and I even tried to hide from Him. It was killing me; bit by bit my soul was withering.

I spent all those years knowing all the right answers about everything, convincing everyone I was all good. But at no point did I know what I *believed*. I knew answers, but not reality. I knew cognitive truth, but not experiential truth. I was an internal mess. I knew right and wrong. I knew Jesus and His saving work. I knew my need for a savior and grace. But I didn't believe these things. I didn't know them like I know my wife or my children—real, experiential, proven. And so, after twenty years as a Christian, sin took over my heart and then my life. It nearly cost me my marriage. It did cost me that job. I was broken. All because I knew answers about everything but didn't truly know what I believed. All because what I showed the world was "right" but inside me was a whole lot of wrong.

It is only grace that has restored me. It was the awful power of God's grace that peeled back layer after layer of hypocrisy, my onion self, to expose my heart to what I knew answers about but truly needed to *believe*. It wasn't the first time I had fallen, and it wasn't the first time God had exposed my sin and His grace, but the other times I had moved on, lesson unlearned. So He peeled me to save me.

More than anything I want my breaking to be the freeing of others. If you are a PK, your answers don't mean anything. They are nothing unless they are based in something you believe, something on which you can base your whole life and hope. If you are a pastor, you must know that your children are layered beings of confusion. Pray they aren't like me but that they see what is *real* and hold fast to it. If you are a church member, a friend of the pastor's family, just pray. This is a knot that cannot be easily untangled. It takes the miraculous to do so, the power of God.

The Politician

Politicians have a remarkable ability to answer questions without really answering them. They can wriggle out of tight spots with just a bit of rhetoric and a healthy dose of charm. When one is done speaking with a gifted politician, he is left with a positive impression and little substance. That's not unlike speaking with certain PKs.

> "The path of least resistance was to follow the rules. I was, however, legalistic, pharisaical, and hypocritical. I thought I was somehow better and 'more spiritual' than other kids at school and church who did not seem to care so much about doing right."
>
> —Matthew Weathers, PK

One of the greatest defense mechanisms a PK can develop is the ability to sound good without risking or revealing anything of substance. When I say "greatest," I don't mean it's commendable—just that it works exceptionally well. A PK has to navigate a life full of questions and scrutiny in the same way a politician does, so what do we do? We learn to answer questions and deflect probing without exposing ourselves. But what makes this so remarkable is that it isn't obviously defensive. It isn't stiff-arming or rude. We leave questioners feeling engaged and respected, like we gave them exactly what they wanted.

Some PKs do this through humor and witty repartee. (I like to think I fit this category. If I don't, you can keep it to yourself. I enjoy my delusions of being funny.) Making people laugh or spinning their heads with a play on words is a perfect deflection from the topic at hand. Banter is a gift, but it can also be a defense mechanism. It gives the impression of likability without leaving anything of substance.

Being a question asker works well too. Someone comes at the PK with a personal question, and she just politely turns it around.

"How have your devotions been?" says the asker. "Just fine," the PK says. "But how are *yours*?" Nothing revealed. Questioner engaged kindly. Questioner feels respected and like the PK truly cares. Done and done.

It isn't at all hard to see the problems this causes. Relationships are built on authenticity and trust, two ingredients entirely missing from the politician-PK. More importantly, healthy relationships are essential in determining and developing identity. For a PK, whose identity is a muddle of questions, keeping people at arm's length simply exacerbates the problem. No one else knows what's really going on in our hearts and lives, and neither do we. We are a pleasant public face and a roiling mess inside. But who would know that if we don't let them?

The Chameleon

The chameleon is a creature known for its ability to blend into its surroundings, to camouflage itself by changing its own skin color. God has given this lizard a unique ability to protect itself by hiding nearly anywhere. Blending, fitting in, seamless transition from one context to another—these are all traits many PKs develop to survive the threatening demands of life.

Unlike the politician who is an attention-getting force of personality, the chameleon slides from context to context with far less fanfare. She is always present but doesn't seek to stand out. She knows just the balance of interaction and separation to be able to blend. If the situation is boisterous, she will toss in a joke or two to fit in, laugh with others but less loudly, yet she will never force her way to the center of attention. In times of solemn prayer she will "amen" and "mm-hmm" with everyone else, and she will speak out in brief prayers, but even those will be innocuous—appreciated but not remembered.

The chameleon knows how to treat the elderly with respect and make the babies smile. She can converse with anyone, welcome newcomers, and sing out in the worship service. There isn't a churchy behavior that she hasn't mastered, and nobody is the wiser. She blends perfectly; she is exactly what everyone wants. The mission of the chameleon, unspoken and likely unnoticed even by herself, is to be what a situation demands. She can lead a bit, follow a lot, and always fit in.

But what is she really? Does she even know? Her only target her whole conscious life has been to be whatever the situation calls for. What are her unique gifts? What does she like or dislike? What does she believe? All anyone knows of the chameleon is that she is a gifted adapter and actress, if they've even noticed that.

Even worse, the chameleon very likely doesn't know the answers to those questions herself. She has suspicions and feelings. She has internal reactions to situations, people, and teachings. But all she knows how to do is make the situation go smoothly, to be part of it, to fit in. She is nothing but a walking reaction, even though her heart yearns for more and knows it's out there. She wants to be unique, to be bold, or maybe to be quiet and unassuming. She wants to wrestle through hard questions instead of just offering the "right" answers. She wants to figure out her own beliefs instead of how to reflect the beliefs of others.

The chameleon has never had the chance to sit with the reality of Jesus and learn what it means to be His disciple. She is a disciple of circumstance. Maybe she doesn't even want to get too close to

Jesus because His followers have a tendency to stand out. So Jesus is part of her life but not the center of it. He is a flavor, a subject of conversation, but not her identity. She is identified only by what is happening around her and how well she blends in.

The Rebel without a Cause

As hard as the politician and the chameleon try to be smooth, to fit in, to please others, the rebel tries equally hard to defy all that. He sees other PKs, maybe even his own siblings, and scoffs at their efforts to be good. He wants no part of it. It's all foolishness to him. It isn't always clear what the rebel's motivation is, except that he knows what he isn't. He isn't the good kid, the politician, or the chameleon. More than anything, he isn't what everyone wants him to be. He refuses to be that, not ever.

It is difficult to define the rebel except to say that he is contrary. He refutes what his parents teach, bucks the expectations of the church, and spits on the lifestyle associated with the good PK. On the surface it simply looks like his goal is to make his parents miserable—and he succeeds, with a bullet. He makes Mama cry and Daddy fume. He rattles the elders and deacons and shocks the old women. He won't cooperate with the youth pastor or listen to the college pastor. He is simply against everything his parents want.

The big question asked about the rebel PK is "Why?" Why does he act this way? Why does he make life so hard on everyone? Why does he reject his parents' teaching and flaunt his revolt so blatantly? What does he want?

The primary difference between the rebel and the politician or the chameleon is that the rebel has recognized the hypocrisy and refuses to participate. He won't be something he doesn't believe in. He won't act the part to make others happy. He sees the inconsistency, the phoniness, and the hollowness and wants nothing to do with it. Why should he be what he is asked to be if he doesn't believe it? Forget the church and its stupid expectations.

What the rebel doesn't realize is that he is not so dissimilar to the politician or the chameleon after all. Just because he has decided *not* to be something doesn't mean he is any closer to knowing what or who he is. He is just as driven by expectations as his fellow nonrebel PKs—he simply chooses the opposite path from them. When they turn left and concede to please others, he turns right and refuses to do so. It doesn't matter where that right turn leads. He will take it. All his turns and steps are determined by trying not to be something, not by any definitive pursuit of anything. He will end up who-knows-where because he has simply sought to avoid being something. The rebel lacks identity just as much as his goody-two-shoes counterpart PKs.

Who Is This Jesus?

A more important identity question faces PKs than "Who am I?" and that is "Who is Jesus?" He is the key to decipher this mess. At first blush, answering this question seems simple. After all, PKs know more about Jesus than almost anyone. But that's just it—we know all *about* Jesus, but that doesn't mean we actually know Him. We know all the answers to all the questions, all the parables, every beatitude, and a list of His miracles too. We know Luke 2 by heart and the names of the men who carried Jesus's cross and laid Him in the tomb. (Simon of Cyrene and Joseph of Arimathea, respectively;

that's a solid Bible Baseball double.) Jesus is a ubiquitous presence in the upbringing of a PK.

This ubiquity seems like it would be an asset. What could be better for a soul than being inundated with Bible teaching and words about Jesus all the time? With that kind of upbringing, PKs ought to be super-Christians, so why all this identity crisis and rebellion stuff?

> "Finding God was the greatest challenge. Being raised in an atmosphere where God was ministry, vocation, and hobby makes it hard to be amazed by the gospel. Being raised where life is always about showing God to a group makes it hard to see God individually."
>
> —Jeremy Noel, PK

Being around Jesus-related teaching, literature, and events all the time makes Jesus rote in the minds and hearts of PKs. Rote is mundane. When Jesus becomes mundane, He ceases being life-changing and life-giving. In the case of many PKs, He never was either of these; by their estimation, He was just a character in an overtold story. Instead of Savior and Lord, He becomes any number of other things, most of which take on the character of those who represent Him in the church.

Jesus is Dad's boss. Jesus is the job. Jesus is boring. Jesus is all seriousness and no fun. Jesus is judgmental. Jesus is a religious blowhard. Jesus is legalistic. Jesus is a soft-spoken wimp. Jesus cares about poor people and despises the rich. Jesus cares about rich people and ignores the poor. Jesus is a hard-line teacher with no room for questions or doubts. Jesus is white. And so on. Every one of these descriptions is a reflection of a church culture or a caricature of a single aspect of who Jesus is. But none of them *is* Jesus, and if you add them all up, you get something resembling a psychotic monster, not a God-man Savior.

Knowing the real Jesus is the only way a PK can sort through his own identity issues. Without the knowledge of Jesus's humanity—real, compassionate, struggling, tempted humanity—the PK can't relate to Him. Without knowledge of the infinite grace poured out in Jesus's blood on the cross, the PK has no hope for anything. Instead, he has fear and suppressed doubts and struggles. PKs need to know that Jesus gives room for questions, forgives sins, loves people who don't know Him or love Him back, doesn't leave or abandon or crush out of vengeance or spite. We need to know that even as He is profoundly loving He is profoundly just and powerful. He is no mere cupcake or huggable teddy bear. He is powerfully gentle, majestically soft, lovably strong, and comfortingly forceful. We need to get to know Jesus as real, not as concept or boss or job or anything else.

Only when Jesus becomes real to a PK can she begin to figure out what she is, who she is. It is in the freedom of Jesus's overwhelming love that the PK can break out of false expectations and see what makes Jesus happy. No longer does the outside pressure define her. No more does she feel the need to fake it, to hide, to blend, or to rebel. She *knows* what is real—or rather who is real—and He is wonderful. Only in the person of Jesus is there power enough to free the PK to know who she is.

Chapter 5

WHAT A
PK NEEDS
MORE THAN
ANYTHING

With all the difficulties laid out thus far, one wonders how a PK can come to know Jesus. We have the best teaching by nearly any standard—shoot, our dads have degrees stacked on degrees. We spend more man-hours (or child-hours) in church than anyone else. We learn catechisms, prayers, trivia, confessions, Scripture passages, and a few C. S. Lewis quotes to top it off (mud pies in a slum, anyone?). But this is not what makes Jesus real to a PK. A PK needs Jesus shown to him, not just told to him.

PKs grow up with lessons of Jesus flying past us at every turn. But because of our own identity issues, because of the expectations placed on us by the church, we have enormous difficulty in actually relating to Jesus. If these are His people, why are they so difficult? They are called "the body of Christ," but if they are part of Jesus, then why do they look and act so little like Christ? Or is it that they do act like Christ and He isn't someone who is very likable after all? It's confusing enough to make one want to give up, which many PKs do.

> "I struggled with seeing a pattern of behavior in the home and hearing something different being propounded and preached in the pulpit."
>
> —Jonathan Holmes, PK

For many PKs, there is a serious disconnect between what they see from their own dad and what he says about Jesus. Jesus is loving, gracious, forgiving, and sacrificial. Dad is none of those things. Jesus accepts you as you are. Dad demands more. Jesus forgives sins. Dad harps on them. Jesus makes us white as snow. Dad finds every stain. Jesus loves children and is joyful. Dad holes up in his office and keeps a stern countenance. So what are the lessons PKs learn of Jesus? Who knows?

If everything described thus far seems daunting for the PK, and maybe more so for his parents, it is. No man is adequate to the task of a father. I have two daughters whom I love dearly, but as often as I think of how dear they are to me, I also think, *What am I doing?* Dads put on a good face, but most of us spend most of the time scrambling to figure out what it means to be a good father. Without grace from both God and our families, we would be lost.

No man is adequate to be a pastor either, especially not as the position of pastor is viewed today: One man bearing the spiritual well-being, financial well-being, theological education, and marital and familial health of an entire church. While being responsible to care for his own family. I'd say that's a job no person is up for, not alone, not without profound grace. And that is the key to all this: grace. That is what the PK needs to see, to know more than anything.

PKs Need to See the Need

Everyone is a sinner. Everyone needs forgiveness for their sins. Every PK knows these statements (if not the realities). They are drilled into our heads starting early. But what do they mean to the PK? What does it look like to be a sinner in need of forgiveness?

Like most kids, we learn reality from watching our parents. And like the old saying goes, actions speak louder than words. We hear "sinners need grace," but what do we see? Too often it is a lack of need, or rather a lack of admission of need. Too often we see parents who strive to present themselves as the flawless heroes they can never be (for us or the church) instead of the flawed, idiosyncratic, weird, and sinful people they really are. As we grow older and more aware, these unmatched states of being come into stark relief. We see sins and mistakes and shortcomings but hear no admissions or apologies. And so our understanding and acceptance of sin and grace are broken.

What the PK needs is parents who not only admit to being sinners but actually admit to *sins*. It is far more powerful for a child to see his parents admitting, apologizing for, and working to correct real, actual sins. When a father refers to himself as a sinner and says he needs grace but doesn't make a habit out of admitting and apologizing for specific failings, he mixes up his kids. PKs see the lost tempers, the harsh words, the overwork, the pride, the gossip. We know what sins our dad commits, but if he doesn't admit to them, we can lose respect for him. We also fail to learn to recognize sins in our own lives, and even if we do see them, we won't admit them. Why should we? Dad doesn't.

> "I believe if ministry parents preached grace and transparency from the pulpit and inside the home, the pressures would be lifted."
>
> —Jordan Taylor, PK

Add up all those responses and there is an even worse potential outcome: PKs never gain a sense of their own need for grace. We may have deep guilt because of an innate recognition of badness or incompleteness. We may suffer from all the identity issues we explored in the last chapter. But none of this adds up in the PK's mind to *I need the grace of Jesus to fix all this*. Grace is nothing to the PK who has never seen anyone desperate for it. It is just a word, a concept maybe. But it is not a source of life and identity.

However, grace, the undeserved favor of God through Jesus, *is* the source of life and personhood and identity. I wasn't able to see my need for that until I was out of college, not really, not fully. And that was only when grace smashed over me like a breaker at Big Sur. It threw me around and rattled me and turned me head over heels. And it washed away all the layers of sin and self-dependence I had built through years of "not needing" grace. If I had seen my need earlier and thrown myself into the waters of grace, I would have been able to enjoy the surf instead of being battered by it.

PKs Need to See the Grace Itself

Sin is a big deal. The Bible makes that clear. Sin is what separates us from God, and there's nothing worse than that. Sin induces guilt, feeling bad about something we've done. Guilt can lead to repentance, or it can drive people further from God and those they love when it morphs into the ugliness of shame. Shame is guilt compounded so many times over that it becomes unbearable and begins to shape us. It is guilt as an identity, the feeling that I *am* bad because of all the things I have done. Sin turns everything on its head; it makes truth look like a lie and makes lies look appealing. It turns friends into enemies and harmful people into desirable ones. Sin makes good habits boring and loathsome and turns destructive habits into alluring ones. It seeks to own our minds and souls and actions. And this is true for everyone, PK or otherwise.

I started this book explaining that PKs are normal people, which means, among many other things, we are sinners. But as we've seen, the pressures and demands on a PK aren't normal, and when you put a flawed person dealing with the same struggles against sin under uncommon pressure, she often crumbles or twists. The pressures of being a PK are almost unavoidable, but there is one protection from them, and that's grace—active, expressive, consistent, continual grace—from our parents and churches.

> "The best way I could think of to help address the pressures of ministry is to let their kids see that even pastors are not perfect and the only hope of living a life 'for God' is through surrender and trust."
>
> —Jon Stepan, PK

It is the grace of God that allows anyone to make headway in the struggles to overcome sin. It is the gift of the Holy Spirit that enables followers of Jesus to make good decisions in the face of temptations, and the Spirit lives in anyone who has acknowledged Jesus as their Savior, as the one and only means to get right with God. The ultimate grace was the sacrifice of the perfect, sinless Jesus for the sake of all humanity to give up His heavenly glory, live a human life, and agonizingly die on the grotesque cross so that we would not have to face eternal punishment for dishonoring the perfect God. It was grace because no one else could do it and no one in history deserved it, yet Jesus did it anyway. It was grace because it was done by the one man whom death could not hold. It was grace because it was *given* to all as the means of peace, hope, and relationship with God.

Such grace is profound, yet it is obscured from so many PKs. So many of us feel the judgment of the church and of our parents, even as they preach grace. Jesus washed the feet of betrayers and deniers, ate meals with hookers and cheats, used the last of His breaths to pardon a thief and plead mercy on His murderers. This is grace. Why is it so hard to find for so many PKs?

Even as Jesus showed such mercy to the dregs of society, He was hard on one set: the self-righteous prigs who burdened others and withheld grace. These were the people who made it harder for others to draw near to God or know Him. They presented God as a being who was unattainable and often undesirable. They created barriers between "sinners"—as they called those they deemed lesser—and God, when in fact they were no better.

Such is the experience of so many PKs even if it's not explicit. They find themselves facing a series of barriers between them and God, between them and forgiveness. Sometimes these are from the church at large, but often they are parental. Pastors can create the greatest obstacles between their children and God.

Obstacles to Grace

Extra Rules

Sometimes the *extra* in *extra rules* means rules unique to the PK that differ from rules for their peers, as we saw in chapters 2 and 3. Just as often, though, these rules are extrabiblical with little or no explanation. Better than plain rules are principles. Instead of saying

"No R-rated movies," it is worth defining what kind of content ought to be avoided and why. There is a big difference between *Schindler's List* and *American Pie*. Principles give explanation and fit multiple situations. Rules are rigid, don't always apply, and create frustration.

This is not to say children don't need rules, but all rules should have a genuine explanation for the benefit of the follower. Otherwise, they are holiness hoops through which the PK jumps to get to God. What the PK needs most is to see *why* and *how* these rules will bring him closer to God. Without this explanation, rules can become hollow, meaningless, hypocritical, and burdensome.

Black-and-White Everything

Not everything is right or wrong, true or false, yes or no. The PK needs some maybes and sort ofs. If every question is answered in black and white and every decision judged as right or wrong, the PK never learns to make value decisions. In fact, he never learns values at all. He just learns to dance the morality two-step and avoid getting out of step with what's "good" or "true." If every question is given a concrete answer and no room is left for exploration or doubt, the PK is forced to either acquiesce or bury his doubts where they can fester and rot his faith.

Christianity is full of mystery and unknown depths because God is deeply mysterious. That's why this faith is so amazing. If everything can be explained in clear terms, the impression the PK is given is that Christianity is a nicely buttoned-up, black-and-white construct. Instead of being wonderful, mind expanding, and moving, it becomes discardable because it is no longer profound.

False Forgiveness

To forgive is to release someone from a debt owed and to wash away a stain—permanently. Forgiveness is no mere expression of "It's okay"; it is a decision to let go of the wrong done so both the forgiver and the forgiven can be free and relationship can be restored. Partial forgiveness is not forgiveness at all. In fact, that's a nonsense phrase because partial forgiveness is false forgiveness.

False forgiveness is the outward expression of it without the requisite actions and attitudes. It might exhibit itself as coldness or strain. It might be a closing off of communication or unexplained changes to expectations or rules. (Sometimes expectations need to be changed when trust is broken, but these should always be clearly explained in the context of true forgiveness.) Often, though, it is the regular dredging up of past failures. This might be as "object lessons" or "reminders." I've even heard pastors bring up the past wrongs of their kids *in order to* point out the grace they think their children overlooked. All this does is rip the heart out of that initial expression of forgiveness. Forgiveness chooses to forget, to set aside a memory, and chooses to restore. Anything less than this is false.

Lack of Empathy

As I have connected with dozens of PKs, I have often asked the question "Do you think your parents understood the struggles you had or the pressures you faced?" The only PKs who answer yes, their parents understood, are those whose parents are also PKs. Without fail the rest say no. Most pastors simply do not understand what a PK's life is like unless they have been there and done that—and even then it's easy to forget. To really understand, the pastor needs empathy.

Empathy is the ability to put yourself in another person's situation, the effort to understand that person's perspective. All kids need this from parents, and almost all parents are kind of terrible at it (I say this as a parent). However, PKs in particular need parents (and churches) to be empathetic. For all the reasons listed in the previous chapters, PKs face significant pressures, realities that make the challenges of learning to make decisions that much harder and the consequences of mistakes that much stiffer. We need parents who strive to put themselves in our heads and "get" us. We need parents who remember their own idiocy as children and young adults and give an extra measure of grace.

Like all kids, PKs need discipline for willful disobedience. But parents or leaders need to provide an example of care with it, not just a sermon or lecture or scolding. As a whole, PKs are greatly misunderstood, and we feel it. That's why, in part, I wrote this book. That misunderstanding, even by our parents, leads to a mess of potentially negative responses to straight discipline. The lack of effort to understand, to walk a mile in our shoes, cheapens any biblical message. It becomes a message thrown at us instead of one shared with us.

The PK as Job Qualification

Of all the obstacles to grace I have described, parents who gauge their children's behavior based on job title is the most particular to PKs. In two of the pastoral epistles, 1 Timothy and Titus, qualifications are given for pastors and elders. In 1 Timothy 3:4 they are phrased this way: "He must manage his own household well, with all dignity keeping his children submissive." Without getting into all the hermeneutical whatnots and wherefores, this verse opens a serious can of worms for the pastor's family.

The pastor is commanded to keep his kids submissive. Well now, I know plenty of disruptive and unsubmissive little pastor's kids. And what happens if his teenage son rebels in a public way? (The private rebellions are much more easily swept under the rug.) Or if his daughter leaves the faith and becomes a lesbian? Is there an age limit on this? Is the pastor safe if the rebellious child is out of the house? What happens if his grown child is fired from his job for unethical practices or gets his girlfriend pregnant or, even worse, commits some criminal act? What if it's less blatant rebellion but rather a slow drift away from the church and following Jesus? I know PKs who have been or done all of these. I have done some of them myself.

So I tell you this: The pressure of keeping my father in his job by being "submissive" is not something that makes me (or any other PK) want to follow Jesus. The tacit reminder that our rebellion may cost Dad his job is not an expression of grace leading to repentance and restoration. It is a cause for resentment. Our rebellion is an expression of need, a searching for something to fulfill us. It is wrong, yes, but that is not resolved by reminding us of the difficulty Dad is having with the elders because of us. That's just too bad. We need many things to help us, but such a reminder is not one of them.

"Show grace and mercy to your children by living it
out to them daily. I think it would make it easier for

them to communicate openly with you about what
is truly on their hearts."

—Chriselda Dirrim, PK

What Grace Looks Like

Grace Is Holistic

Grace is never less than forgiveness, empathy, and a willingness to let
PKs question and fail, but it is much more than that too. It is more,
even, than a pastor exhibiting and expressing his own need for grace.
In all, grace must be holistic, shaping and tempering all areas of life,
like it was for Jesus.

Grace shaped Jesus's entire life, from His setting aside glory to
become a mortal man to His savage death and glorious overcoming
of it. But where grace is seen in its most relatable way is in His daily
interactions with people. What was it that drew scheming, devious
Zacchaeus to Jesus and then to repentance? What was it that bound
the formerly demon-possessed Mary Magdalene to Him with such
loyalty that she risked her own welfare to be present at His death and
His resurrection? It was the power of perfect and consistent—that is,
holistic—grace. Jesus's grace was so profound that it unlocked hearts,
evicted evil, and won sinners to Him time and again. Sometimes it
won them more than once. Think of Peter, the disciple who became
the denier and was won by grace to become the rock on which Jesus
built His church.

PKs struggle with grace. We have seen it is so often skewed or
hidden or distant. But Jesus showed everyone the markers of true
grace. Such markers are what can make grace real to the jaded and

damaged PK. We need these from our parents and our churches alike. And we need to believe them and participate in them too. Grace is given, and thus grace must be received.

Grace Cares about Life and Soul

True grace cares deeply about the inner workings (or not-workings) of a person. It cares about the good and the bad. It cares because it loves, with no self-serving agenda. This is soul care, the kind of care that is eager to bear burdens and share pain. This is the grace that PKs so often feel is absent as people judge our behavior and how we meet expectations. This is the grace that also cares about the little things that aren't really little—the hobbies and interests and crushes and romances. This grace engages life from the day-to-day to the eternal because it all matters, it all makes up the person of the PK, and because this grace truly cares.

This grace shows that it cares by interacting with the mundane as well as the eternal. It isn't always pushing to get to the soul or trying to pray. It asks questions and listens to answers. It is interested in me, what I do for fun, what I'm struggling with at work, my funny stories about my kids, a baseball game I went to, and the rest of my everyday life. It is interested because it recognizes that all this makes up life and all this is a gateway to my soul.

Grace Assumes Nothing

Assumptions create a tide against which the PK cannot swim. In chapters 2 and 3 we looked at some assumptions about PKs and at expectations placed on them. The expectations inform the assumptions—the PK is a perfect angel, Bible scholar, theologian, future superpastor or missionary—and the assumptions feed the expectations. It's a vicious cycle. Grace looks at the PK and sees a person. Grace is aware of the weakness and sinfulness within and assumes nothing about the current mental or spiritual state of the PK. This balance between awareness and lack of assumption allows the PK to speak freely and be free. Grace allows the PK to be who she really is without burdening her with assumptions of spiritual superiority and health.

Grace also knows that what's on the surface isn't what's really going on in the heart of the PK, so it knows to gently ask and prod to find out who the real person is and what the real beliefs are. And when it finds out that what the church sees is not really who the PK is, grace is not surprised or offended. And so it creates an opportunity for the PK to be genuine.

Grace Has No Unfair Expectations

True grace expects a PK to be only what God made him to be, not some formulation of ministerial perfection fabricated by the collective stupidity of the church. It does not heap burdens of extra morality or spirituality on the PK. This is not to say that grace has no expectations. To expect nothing of someone is to not care about him. Instead, grace has only the fairest expectations—those that any believer is called to. It expects a PK to try to honor Jesus but to fail at it. It expects the PK to try, fail, and cry out for help. And then it lends a helping hand.

Grace also expects the best and expects the PK to pursue the best. It doesn't expect any particular track, but it does expect the PK to become something. It expects the gifts the PK has to be used in good ways, so it helps the PK see those gifts and learn to develop them. One of the hardest things for PKs, and this was certainly the case for me, is to figure out who we are and how we are gifted. Holistic grace recognizes this and teases out those gifts until they are real, visible, and being put to use.

> "They both really helped me realize that my talents and passions were in the business/entrepreneur realm. It was because of my dad's insight and encouragement that our team and I have just launched a start-up business. And everything I do through my full-time job and where I live and where I play is all my ministry. It's all mission."
>
> —Angela Jackson, PK

Grace Will Walk Any Mile It Asks Another to Walk

I grew up knowing of Jesus as God and man. I knew all the stories of His life. But it was not until I began to understand the depth of Jesus's humanity that I began to love Him truly. For me, it was easy to think of Jesus as God—perfect, overcoming death, sinless. But it was hard to understand that He walked this earth facing the same temptations I do, being hurt by others like I have been, being raised by imperfect parents like I have been, having expectations heaped on Him like I have had. Well, that's not right—the expectations heaped on Him were to be Messiah, Redeemer, and Savior of God's people. That's a fair bit more than I have dealt with. Jesus walked every mile He has asked me to walk. He faced sin and didn't participate. He had relationships and didn't hurt others or retaliate when they hurt Him. He had family and didn't let their drama or screwups make Him bitter or distant or hateful. That is grace incarnated.

That is the kind of grace PKs need to see from our parents and the church. No one can truly walk in our shoes, but people can incarnate the grace of Jesus. We need to see more of it in all of life.

Grace Is No Respecter of Persons

The phrase "respecter of persons" is an old-fashioned phrase, a bit archaic even.[7] Those of us who grew up steeped in Bible teaching and terminology likely recognize it, but it has definitely fallen out of the vernacular. Being a "respecter of persons" means something different than having respect for people. Grace has respect for people, but it does not view one as more innately valuable than another—that is to be a "respecter of persons." Grace treats all people as equally created by God and equally valuable. The PK is no better than others and no worse. Sometimes this means grace must cut the PK down to size when he gets too big for his britches.

More than once I have had my big head deflated by a pointed gracious word from a good friend, reminding me that my last name doesn't make me better than anyone else. I remember distinctly a Sunday afternoon when I was seventeen. Shae McCowan, a volunteer leader with our youth group, took me out to TGI Friday's for lunch and had a pointed conversation with me—well, he talked and I mostly listened (which was rare for me). "Barnabas, you have all the potential in the world to be a great leader. But you can be a real punk. You need to accept the responsibility to lead. People look up to you. Own it." That was the gist of the conversation. He cut me down and lifted me up. And he paid no attention to my last name or to my being a PK. I have never forgotten it.

Sometimes, though, grace means lifting the PK up from the pit of frustration and guilt he has fallen into because of persistent failure to live up to others' expectations. This grace keeps an even keel with a concrete evaluation of people: people are ugly because of sin but beautiful because they are God's handiwork and redeemed by Jesus. It reminds the PK of whichever of those truths he needs.

Grace Sees What God Could Make Someone

Because grace recognizes that all people are the work of a Creator, uniquely designed to reflect Him, it also sees the potential in each person to be that unique reflection. Grace doesn't look at PKs as reflectors of their parents or icons for their churches. It doesn't see us as chips off the old block. It doesn't have a plan for each PK to become anything but rather looks for the marks of God's creativity on him and sees them as road signs pointing to what the PK could be. These markers might be unique gifts and passions, standout qualities. And when grace sees them, it sees what they can become—not how they fit in a grand plan to make the PK into something to please his parents or his church.

But grace also knows that it is only God who can form the PK into anything at all, so it does not harangue, harass, or manipulate the PK. Grace will seek to assist and encourage rather than direct and command. It will point out strengths and possibilities rather than command actions and expect results. This is especially applicable as the PK grows older—through the adolescent years and beyond—and begins to seek independence. This is what I missed out on most growing up and even through college. I came away with no ideas of what God made me to be, what He gifted me with. I knew I wasn't dumb and that I was capable of lots of things, but what things? PKs need gracious guidance and freedom from manipulation in order to become the persons we are uniquely designed to be as reflections of God.

Hope

Too often what derails a PK is hopelessness. She feels hopeless to live up to expectations, hopeless to be what Dad wants her to be, hopeless to figure out who Jesus really is, hopeless to figure out who she really is. Grace provides hope because grace provides chances. If she fails, it is not a tally against her in the record of the cosmic scorekeeper; it is merely a failure, a chance to learn and grow. Grace provides the opportunity and motivation to keep going, keep searching, keep trying. It provides the courage to be different than her parents or her church and the hope that she will become what God made her to be rather than what others want her to be.

In the movie *Shawshank Redemption*,[8] Andy Dufresne writes in a letter to Red, "Hope is a good thing, maybe the best of things, and no good thing ever dies." Hope must have a foundation for it to be real, and the foundation of true hope is grace—the grace of God through Jesus and that same grace exhibited by followers of Jesus. This is the hope of salvation, the hope of identity, the hope of morality, the hope of happiness. Without grace there is no hope, but with it there is no shortage.

Chapter 6

PASTOR AND
CHILD

"Families were sacrificed on the altar of ministry, and the pressures of life burned both to the ground."

—Matthew Weathers, PK

"The best shepherds shepherd those closest to them in the Kingdom. You can never be a good pastor when you can't pastor your physical family, I don't care how 'successful' your ministry may be."

—Angela Jackson, PK

The grace described in the last chapter is a grace PKs need from all sides—from the church at large as well as the nuclear family. I gave categories of grace, filters through which people can press their actions and motivations to sift out gracelessness. In this chapter I will address the pastor and spouse, the parents of PKs. Certain expressions of grace are particular to the pastor and don't apply to the larger church. Such expressions are personal, often intensely so. The relationship between pastor and child is defined by these expressions or their absence. In fact, without the expressions of grace that follow, a healthy relationship cannot exist between pastor and child.

Be a Parent, Not a Pastor

Pastors have often been encouraged to "pastor their families." I understand the sentiment such exhortation carries. It speaks to the spiritual care of spouse and children and being a good leader in the home. In short, it is given in the spirit of the real meaning of *pastor*—a shepherd, a caretaker of a flock. Despite the best intentions of such an instruction, though, it is bad advice. The problem lies in the functional, cultural definition of *pastor* and the expectations that lie on the role.

In the Western church the role of pastor has taken on responsibilities and definitions it ought not. The pastor is seen as the spiritual burden bearer for an entire congregation. He is the prophetic voice of authority, the nearly infallible voice of God. He is the answer man for questions on topics ranging from sex to stewardship to sanctification. He is the figurehead of a religious institution, and often this means he is a political pundit too. He must be an expert accountant, theologian, psychologist, marketer, strategist, and orator. In short, he must exhibit every spiritual gift God intended to be dispersed throughout the entire church. The cultural expectations on pastors are mostly unbiblical, entirely impractical, and generally downright stupid. We each expect the pastor to meet our particular need with expediency and wisdom. It is an untenable situation, a burden no man can bear.

Many pastors haven't even given thought to this. They simply go about their lives and ministries trying to meet all these expectations. They view their role as church culture has defined it; they know no other way. Some may buck the expectations or have a subtle sense that something isn't quite right. Others embrace the expectations and begin to think of themselves as able to fulfill all the demands of the role. These often view themselves as CEOs or develop "god complexes" where they can find or be the solutions to any difficulty. Still others just wither and get emptied out into a discouraged husk of a minister. The best response is from the pastor who realizes his own limitations, is honest about them, and simply does what he can to minister to his congregation while getting help to do what he can't.

So to say that a pastor must "pastor his family well" is functionally—because of church culture—to ask him to be Superman for the church and Superman at home. This is bad for everyone involved. Only by grace can a man be even a decent man, and no man can be super.

Pastors, your children need a parent, not a pastor. They don't need you to bring the expectations of your job into the home. They *know* you're not Superman. They know what you're bad at. And what they really need is you to just be you, the parent, with all your weaknesses and foibles. So the best response to the advice to "pastor your family well" is to realize your limitations, be honest about them, do what can be done, and get help with what can't. Just don't try to be a pastor at home.

> "I think the big thing [in helping me deal with the pressure of being a PK] was my dad being my dad, not my pastor."
>
> —Tyler Braun, PK

Family Is Your Calling

The position of pastor is understood to be a "calling," not just a job. *Calling* is a loaded term, one that carries more weight than *career* or *occupation* or even *ministry*. It is a term that can set the role apart as something that God has uniquely placed a person in. A problem arises, though, when "calling" elevates the position above where it ought to be. Let me explain.

I believe in callings. I believe God pulls people toward particular positions and occupations. I do not, however, believe that the pastoral calling is a higher calling than any other. Unique? Yes. But not higher. God calls people to sell bonds, publish books, build houses, teach literature, trade stocks, create art, and be pastors. Each of these callings involves a pull toward a role based on specific gifts and passions God has given a person. Each is a singular expression of the image of God and carries the expectation of excellence and doing the work in a way that honors God.[9] Each is unique in the way it declares the image and glory of God. For the pastor, this is done with proclamation, teaching, and example. The pastor is called to teach and to lead, yes, but he is not above those he leads who are called to other roles. Each one needs the others, and all combine to be a fuller representation of the Creator.

What happens when the calling of pastor is elevated beyond where it ought to be is that he gains both the freedom and the expectation to be and do things others ought not. Since the pastor is seen as doing "God's work" in some unique way, it becomes okay for him to work seventy- and eighty-hour weeks, even though such excess would be frowned upon and maybe even rebuked if the bond salesman did it. Overwork is a cultural norm in America as people seek to "get ahead" in the world (a critique that does not apply to those who work two or three jobs out of necessity). Work has become an idol or a crutch for many, including pastors. Pastors are expected to be available to their congregation at any time of day or night—dinnertime, their daughter's soccer game, school open house, moving their son to college. Missing a day of work, which might mean not preaching on a Sunday, is seen as dereliction of duty rather than simply what it is: family time or vacation.

Many of these expectations come from the outside, the church pressuring pastors. But many are self-imposed. Or maybe pastors simply passively adopt them. No matter what, though, the family suffers.

What pastors need to realize is that their first calling is to their families, not the church. Yes, the church is a calling too, and balancing the two is enormously difficult. As in many other industries, the job does sometimes demand attention in a way that cannot be ignored. But when someone marries and becomes a parent, those people—the family—must come first. It is wrong, sinful, to put us on the sidelines and treat pastoral ministry as if it is the "primary" or "real" calling. Pastors must keep the dual calls in proper relation to one another, as difficult as that may be.

The pastor's family needs the best of his time and energy. As much as possible, we need his full attention and passion. The sermon is not more important than the concerns or crises of wife or children. Stay up late or get up early to finish it. The deacons' meetings are not more important than Little League games. Reschedule the meetings if they are a regular conflict, or maybe delegate their leadership to a trusted coworker. (Having trusted coworkers is a lifeline every pastor needs.) Other people's parenting struggles are not worth more effort than your own, so don't devote all your time to searching for someone else's lost sheep while your own go wandering off a cliff because the shepherd wasn't tending them. The same goes for marital issues.

Pastors, like so many managers and employees in the general workforce, face tasks and demands that cannot be shirked. People supporting their families find themselves bound to particular responsibilities at work, and sometimes these require missing family functions or a delay in dealing with pressing issues. I travel several times a year for my job, and as much as I can, I try not to schedule trips close to any holidays, birthdays, or family events, but sometimes I don't have a choice. It's what the job demands. Pastors must work through these same challenges but with one significant difference: they have more choice in the matter. I travel when my superiors assign me a trip. Pastors often have more leeway because they are the primary decision makers. They may not feel like it ("The people *need* me!" "They specifically asked me to be there."), but they do have leeway. Often pastors can share responsibilities with other church leaders. Other times certain tasks can be delayed so the pastor can have family time. Yes, some crises and meetings are drop-everything-and-go events, but not nearly as many as one would think. Herein lies the importance of balancing the calling. Only the pastor, and maybe his family, can rightly say whether he is successfully caring for his family and prioritizing them, not anyone on the outside. And it is crucial for him to do so.

> "It seems easier to justify absence, harshness, impa-
> tience, and uninvolvement when the justification
> is the lost world, sick saints, and vision meetings."
> —Jeremy Noel, PK

Missing some family time is inevitable in almost any job, especially in emergency services and on-call professions such as doctors or those who own their own businesses. But for those occupations, we recognize it as a problem if this absence becomes the norm, and the pastorate should not be an exception. For pastors, though, absence *is* often the norm, and the "calling" gives them a free pass. It is a double standard, one that ignores the fact that the highest earthly calling is to one's family. Pastors must put their families first, before sermons and elders and congregants and Sunday morning service. Yes, balance is required and it is difficult, but if they do this well, all those other aspects of calling and ministry will be the healthier for it. If they cannot do it, then they ought not be pastors at all.

Put Grace into Practice

Showing grace is done in distinct, individual actions. The grace PKs need is much more than categorical and conceptual. It is timely, personal, incarnated. To be a parent before a pastor is done in the day-to-day moments of life, in particular acts of grace. To follow the calling of family first is a grace to the family, to the PKs. What follows are particular expressions of grace that PKs need from our parents. These actions are the foundation of relationship between pastor and child and can be the difference between a PK who is lost and resentful and one who loves her parents, the church, and Jesus. And sadly, as I've learned from numerous conversations with fellow PKs, they are what is most often missing from a PK's relationship with her parents.

Don't Counsel, Converse

Pastors counsel everyone. An entire church and sometimes even complete strangers come to them for advice. And often this advice is in the form of Scripture. PKs know all this. We know when our parents are giving "pastory" answers. That's not what we want, though. We want parent answers. We want empathy and care and curiosity, not counsel from the book of Romans. When PKs talk with our parents, too often it feels like we are being quizzed for right answers or being felt out for weak spots in our emotions, theology, or worldview. Too often it feels like we are being probed and prodded to find the flaws. That's not conversation. It's what shrinks and teachers and scientists do.

PKs are known of by many but not really known. We want conversation, to open up and share and to be shared with. We need an avenue of communication, not a library of advice. We need to pour out what is boiling in us and overflow with what is bubbling. We need to explore what is really nagging at us. And who better to do this with than our parents? Too rarely are we actually able to do so, though.

Conversation is not conversation without it going both ways. One of the main reasons I felt like I was being counseled growing up was not that my parents failed to listen or didn't have time for me. It was because the conversation didn't start with them or even really include them. When I was little, I didn't hear from them what naughty things they did as children. As I grew, I didn't know what their hardships were as teens, and as a teenager, I really wanted to know that broken hearts or struggles with lust or overwhelming stress was normal and that I could survive. I didn't know the honest struggles they had in relating to God or if they had any at all, so as I got older, I wasn't sure it was safe to unload my questions or doubts. I didn't hear of their struggles with prayer or anger. I didn't hear about their past breakups and heartbreaks. So it didn't feel like a conversation. It felt like I shared, they listened, and I got advice. Until I just stopped sharing.

Quit Praying and Talk to God

PKs know every method and language of prayer that exists. We can beseech with the best of them and sprinkle a little King James into our prayers. We know when to refer to God as "thee" and our friends as "saints" or "brothers and sisters." We can call on Emmanuel, God with us, Abba, Father, King of Kings, Great Physician, Shepherd, Guide, Teacher, Lord, Rabbi, Savior, Creator, Adonai, Messiah and finish it off with a Maranatha for good measure. We can drop a timely "amen" into another person's prayer to show our resonance with it and ice that cake with a hearty "mm-hmm." And above all, we have the "prayer voice." You know, that voice that's a half octave higher and a few decibels softer and comes more from the nose and back of the throat than the actual vocal cords? That's the prayer voice, the one PKs have mastered to add the requisite sincerity to our prayers.

But none of this means we know how to talk to God. I was twenty-seven before I realized just how stupid it is to be afraid to tell God what I'm thinking. He knows my heart. He knows what I'm not saying as much as what I am saying. I was twenty-seven before I realized I could be angry with God and scream and yell if I needed to. Or I could cry. Or sometimes I didn't need to have words at all and I could just sit there with Him and let my hurting, overwhelmed heart do the prayer for me. It has been in just these past few years that I've realized all the prayer constructs I learned growing up don't help me pray, and in fact they hinder me. I have a relationship with God, so now I try to talk to Him instead of praying, at least in the way I knew before.

This is what PKs need to see—parents talking to God, expressing their relationship to God. We don't need praying parents. We need parents who help us realize it's normal to struggle with prayer and that it's worth it to keep going back to God no matter what. We need parents who talk to God with us and show us what that relationship looks like. And we need it to look like a relationship, not a series of form letters, business proposals, or official requests.

Leave Sermons in the Pulpit

PKs hear more sermons in our lives than any humans alive. We get all the ones on Sundays and usually a few at home during the week too. After a while the efficacy of sermons diminishes for us, at least some of us. We need something different. We need the conversation I wrote about just a few paragraphs ago. We need engagement, not lessons.

This is really hard for most of the church to grasp. For them, sermons, especially from a pastor they like, are something to be devoured hungrily on Sundays, digested over the course of the week, and done again in seven days. Many churchgoers listen to more sermons during the week on the radio or via podcast from other preachers around the country. And that is great. I feel that appreciation toward my pastor now, but it took an intentional paring away of all other sermons from my life (podcast, radio, conferences, etc.) to get to the place where I could once again absorb and be blessed by his sermons.

And he isn't my dad. When people ask me about my father's sermons or teaching, I'm ambivalent. I've just had so much of it. I don't dislike it. In fact, I pay very little attention to it. It's common for someone to ask me, "Hey, did you hear what your dad said about …?" Nope, not usually. I don't mean this disrespectfully; I just don't want his sermons. I would rather talk with him.

Sermons at home are even less effective for PKs than those from the pulpit. They are redundant and out of place. Most of the time pastors slip into preaching mode without realizing it. These kitchen sermons are really effective if the goal is to get the PK to tune out, but if the goal is to communicate a point, try something else. Relate to us. Talk with us. Ask questions. Tell stories. And be a little bit self-deprecating about your tendency to preach about anything. Over time this sort of personal communication at home will make the sermons that much more effective and palatable.

Apologize and Repent for Specific Mistakes and Sins

There is no apology so disingenuous and hard to stomach as the one for nothing. "I am sorry if I have offended anyone." "I apologize if I did anything to hurt you." "I am a sinner and have done things or not done things that have caused hurt; I'm sorry." None of these examples is a true apology. They are acknowledgments that someone's feelings got hurt, that's all. And often these are the kinds of apologies pastors give. The pressure on the pastor to be Superman is such that outright apologizing for specific mistakes or sins seems impossible or terrifying. But it's so necessary, especially at home.

Everyone hurts their family members. Everyone loses patience, snaps angrily at a child or spouse, ignores a family member in need, or complains too often. An apology for these acts is exactly what is needed to clear the air and relieve the hurt. Too often, though, the apologies granted—if any—are of the general variety and don't address specific hurts. But these genuine, specific apologies are what PKs need from our parents. We know our parents' flaws better than just about anyone. And when they are not acknowledged and repented of, they are a breeding ground for bitterness.

The repentance aspect is also important. We need to see our parents actively working on their faults, acknowledging failure, and trusting God to help them grow. It is a risk to admit faults or struggles to loved ones; it can be scary to admit being wrong. But without this kind of transparency, a relationship is marked by distance, a lack of trust and intimacy. And that is too often the relationship between pastors and their children. If, however, there is a conscientious admission of fault or of being wrong, a specific apology, and a visible, ongoing effort to change, pastor and child can start to build a context of grace with each other. It is in this context that PKs can feel safe to admit our own guilt and struggles and wrongdoing, because we see what it looks like to do so and what it looks like to be forgiven.

Laugh, Play, and Be Affectionate

My father is a serious man, too much so I think. He isn't good at balancing work and play, study and recreation. But my fondest memories with him are those of backyard Wiffle ball, fishing at Grandma's pond, early morning basketball games with guys from church, getting horsey rides from him, and swimming in the pool near his dad's place in South Carolina. I remember him cheering louder than anyone else at my baseball and football games and playing catch and fielding ground balls from him at Elliot Park. I remember making up new games and contests with him and my older brothers because we simply had to find a way to compete. Those times stand out in my mind with crystal clarity as the best times I had with him. I suspect that during my growing-up years he thought (hoped?) family devotions might have the strongest effect on me, but it was the times of pure, uninhibited fun that etched themselves in my mind most deeply.

To a child, play is love. I felt loved when my dad played with me and took me on adventures. I felt loved when we tromped through the Georgia woods to look for Civil War era ruins or went deep-sea fishing off the coast of South Carolina. I yearned for those times with him. Sure, I grew out of them, but not entirely. I still love it when I can get my dad to a baseball game or when I watch him play make-believe or blocks with my kids.

Pastors can be a serious bunch, inclined to be thinkers and systematic organizers of ideas. That's good for sermons but often useless for relating to children. Actually, let me amend that. That kind of seriousness is good for relating to a scant few people of any age. And *relating* to people is the aim—not communicating effectively or merely spending time, but relationship. (The same holds true for friends and spouses, not only children.) This means connecting with people on the terms that work for them, and most often it is fun and affection that draw people together. For some, fun is competition or fishing. For others, it's conversation over coffee or a shared jigsaw puzzle. Or maybe (for more serious children) it is shared love of exploration and analysis of ideas or places. The reality is that, in the context of relationship, without the connection of recreation and play, the serious message of the gospel becomes heavy, dry, and undesirable. Being fun and affectionate opens doors for eternal things. It makes people feel wanted and welcome and loved. And that creates a context for the most important truths.

Have Hobbies

Pastors, very often, are passionate about their ministry—so passionate, in fact, that it engulfs them. It becomes the sole discernible characteristic of their lives. It never turns off. Their spare time becomes study time, and no matter how much they love studying, this isn't good for anyone. Or maybe the spare time becomes an opportunity to meet with people, to counsel and connect. But this becomes all consuming too.

What a pastor needs is a hobby—golf, reading fiction, music, watching football, biking, woodwork, something, anything. Hobbies are chances to turn the mind off, to rest, to recharge. They are also a buffer between the pastor and the workaholism that plagues so many in ministry.[10] They can be social or they can be solo, but either way the greatest aspect of the hobby is that it makes the pastor more *human*. He becomes able to relate to Joe Average in the third pew because Joe likes biking and football too. Pastors who bury their noses in books and study all the time develop sizzling intellects, produce scintillating sermons and books, but are socially handicapped.

Hobbies provide opportunities for relationships to happen in the most natural way possible, and that is an important aspect of pastoring and an even more important aspect of parenting.

It's not only Joe Average who benefits from the pastor's hobbies; it is the pastor's children too. When parents have interests and passions, they bring their children into them. They offer their children a chance to encounter and try new things. It creates a point of connection between parent and child. My father was excellent at encouraging and enabling my siblings' and my own interests as we grew up. He allowed us to do what we were interested in. He was ever present at our sporting events or recitals with the loudest cheering voice (to the point of getting a yellow card for berating the referees at one of my older brother's soccer games). He made time regularly to play with us after dinner. But there wasn't the sense of being drawn into what he loved. Because what he loved was studying, theology, writing, and preaching—not exactly the hobbies to share with a twelve-year-old. My love of baseball and all things sports just came to me; it wasn't given. My musical tastes happened by accident, not because our home was musical. But to this day, I still yearn to have a shared hobby with my father, something as simple as golf or hiking. Such little things have big meanings.

Have Friends, Not Just Ministry Associates

One of the hardest things for people in ministry is to be known. They are known of widely, but very few friends are in the lives of pastors. Staff members are associates, partners in ministry. The elders and deacons are supporters or companions in a cause. Such groups can easily become a tightly knit web of people working in the same direction with little shared life besides vocational ministry. This has a trickle-down effect. It creates a pseudo-relational culture that can shape and scar PKs.

PKs need to see our parents let their hair down and cut loose with laughter and enjoyment with close friends. We need to see our parents' intensity expressed in preaching, but we also need to see it turned toward other areas of life that have nothing to do with church, theology, or ministry. We need to see our parents turn to a dear friend when crisis hits or grief overwhelms. We need to see a culture, even if it's a small one, of real friendship. (The church as a whole needs the same thing—to have a pastor who has a circle of dear, honest, caring, hard-nosed friends.) Otherwise we become socially stunted and relationally crippled people who struggle to be honest and depend on others for help, comfort, and accountability.

Over the years I have struggled with this. God has given me some of the best friends a person could ask for, and I have failed to treat them the way friends deserve. I haven't been honest with them. I have kept them at bay from parts of my life that were sensitive or ugly or rotten. And this pattern played a role in my greatest struggles and longest falls. I had friends ready and willing to help me, to care for me, or to kick me as needed, and I wouldn't let them in. Instead, those areas of my life rotted and festered and became foul. And in the end I needed those same friends to help me recover from the self-inflicted wounds or the wounds of discipline for my own sins.

Let Me Wonder and Even Wander

Pastors are (mostly) theological people, preachers of the Word, tasked with leading people to Jesus and caring for their souls. And this puts an enormous amount of pressure on them in their own home too. What is reflected by a child who is acting out or rebelling or exploring other beliefs? What will people think if a PK is unsure of the Bible, of the truth his parents are tasked to publicly uphold? More than just the outward pressure is the internal conflict. Pastors function and teach with deep conviction, so for a child to walk away from that or to conflict with it creates a relational rift. In fact, some pastors are so defined by their theology that to depart from it, and I don't even mean departing from the faith, is to build a barrier that can be overcome only by a return to agreement.

This is a horrible mess for PKs. For all the reasons laid out in previous chapters, we are prone to wander and feel the pressure to break out. And like all generations, we are compelled to find our own way in the world—in faith, occupation, identity. We are not uncommon in this, but our parents are uncommonly opposed to our exploration. It seems like a stain on their ministry or parenting. It threatens their position in ministry and status in the eyes of those they lead. Indeed, those are real pressures (even if they are as stupid and misguided as the day is long).

What we need is room to explore. I don't mean that all boundaries and parenting efforts should be forsaken; that would be foolish. But we need emotional and relational space to *be different*. I need to be able to come to God differently than my father does. I need to be able to express faith differently without being corrected or dismissed. I need to be free to have doubts, to speak them without recrimination, and to not know answers. I need to be able to be wrong and then find the right without parental hyperventilating and intrusion in my life. And I need a relationship that is deeper than theological particulars and lifestyle choices. In short, I need a parent's love that runs so deep that no matter what lifestyle or theological choices I make, the relationship holds strong. This is not the same thing as validating all lifestyle choices or decisions; it just means loving deeply no matter what. Pastors need to know that a child's exploration and wandering is not, in most cases, an effort to hurt them. It is an honest seeking of identity, truth, and life.

Give Me the Materials and Let Me Build

I live in the suburbs of Chicago where, like many suburban areas, there are hundreds of housing developments of cookie-cutter houses. As you drive the preplanned streets of these developments and see the beige, gray, and white homes surrounded by saplings and fresh mulch, you get a keen sense of order and sameness. These homes were designed with minimal artfulness and maximum efficiency. The materials used were ordered in bulk and put together according to the same blueprint used on all the neighbors' houses. The streets are winding and fitted with culs-de-sac to make the development appear more like a neighborhood than a preplanned plot of homes. And most of these are comfortable and easy to live in. But they are so life-suckingly *boring*.

The faith handed down to PKs is often just like these housing developments—cookie-cutter, uncreative, preplanned, cheaply built. We live in it for a while until we discover that there are whole worlds out there of culture, creativity, expression, and ideas. These worlds are amazing and confusing to our tree-lined hearts. We don't see how prefab faith fits. And so many PKs abandon the faith they have to live in the brick three-flat of other beliefs or the high-rise apartment of creativity.

What we need is the best possible materials—the strongest and highest quality—for thinking and believing. We don't need a prefab faith but rather the learning and materials to build a strong faith in any context. We need to be taught building skills, not given a prebuilt set of ideas in which to live. We need to be given tools and taught how to use them so that when we run across materials like art, music, movies, sports, work, or relationships, we know how to fashion them into a home that is strong and good.

Fewer PKs would walk away from the faith if we were freely allowed to walk away from our parents' version of faith. If we could build a home of faith that fit our context and our gifts, we would be at home in the faith. But too often we are stuck with a cookie-cutter home of faith and dropped into a context where it doesn't fit or falls apart. And what is left is no home of faith at all. So give us the tools and materials to build anytime anywhere.

We Just Want Parents

I don't know if there is any such thing as a "normal life," but if there is, PKs want it. That means parents who are devoted to the family and are fun and teach us and are available for questions and tears. It means we want a relationship with our parents, not appointments with them. We want to be free to disagree but also to respect them. And we want the same from them.

It also means we don't want perfect parents, or rather we don't expect them. We want parents who care enough to try and admit when they're not succeeding. I am a parent, and it is *hard*. I need grace (lots of it) from God and my children alike. So do pastors, maybe more so than I. All that I have asked of pastors in this chapter is not meant as a burden but rather as an objective, a standard. It is a corrective portrait, a picture of what better PK-pastor relationships could look like. These relationships get jacked up when pastors confuse family and the church.

In the next chapter we'll look at the relationship between pastor, church, and PK. For now, the bottom line is this: PKs just want parents. The greatest grace a pastor can show his children is not being a great pastor; it is being a parent who is fully invested, cares deeply, and shows it as well as he can.

Chapter 7

PARENT
FOR YOUR
CONGREGATION

"I think it is hard to do both [pastor and parent] extremely well because to do both well means time and energy."

—Tyler Braun, PK

American church culture has created a double standard for pastors. They are expected to be dynamic leaders, teachers, counselors, and organizational heads. And one of the job qualifications is also that they be dynamic family men. These two demands would not necessarily be at odds except that both far surpass reality. Pastors are expected to be superior in both roles, even when they are at odds with one another.

It's easy to say "Any good pastor is a good father," but what that actually entails is that the pastor abdicate and delegate certain pastoral duties for the sake of his family. To be a good father, he must necessarily remove himself from some demands of the pastorate. To be a good father, he cannot be the pastor the church at large expects him to be—as Mary Poppins once put it, "practically perfect in every way." Instead, his identity must be as a parent first, for his family's sake and the church's. The church needs to see every pastor as a family man first and pastor second, and so does the pastor's family.

Of course this is an enormous challenge and looks different in different circumstances. The solo pastor of a church of eighty people may feel like he has nobody to lean on. The pastor who heads up a staff of eighty people at a megachurch may feel like the machine will fall apart without him running it. The challenge of being a family man first is the same for both, though, and just as essential to both their churches. I mean it when I call it a challenge. It is complex and hard.

When a pastor misplaces his identity and the pastorate becomes the primary identifying factor, a rift forms between church and family. PKs begin to see the church as our rival for Dad's time and attention. We see him giving his best to other people and pouring out his passion in sermons and vision and strategy and meetings. What we get is the leftovers. When that happens, while he may be seen as a great pastor, he is a flop as a parent.

On the opposite side of the rift is the church. While they may feel they are getting exactly what they need from the pastor, what they are really getting is a hypocrite, intentional or accidental. And they are demanding and empowering this hypocrisy. What the church really needs is a pastor who will drop everything for his family when crisis hits (or ideally, in time to avert a crisis), who consistently makes time for them, and who gives them his best energy.

For pastors, getting to the place in relationship with the church where they can be this available to their families takes time and strong leadership. The church needs to be made to see that they are better off with a pastor who is a good father. Such a shift takes patience and will likely incur frustration on both sides. Thom Rainer, the president of LifeWay, once surveyed the deacons at a church he pastored, asking them how many hours they expected him to devote to eleven different areas of ministry. When he tallied up the responses, the average expectation was 114 hours per week.[11] Darryl Dash, a pastor and blogger, also addressed the expectations he saw placed on pastors. He said congregants expected pastors to work the equivalent of the congregants' work time, commute time, and volunteer hours combined, totaling as many as 65 hours per week.[12] So it's easy to see that leading a church into more reasonable and biblical expectations will take some work and patience. But it must be the goal and it must be attained by degrees, because whether or not they know it, when the church demands the "practically perfect" pastor, they are setting themselves up for disappointment. And they are harming him and his family, sometimes irreparably.

The pastor needs to be a parent at all times—in the pulpit, the board room, the office, at the Little League diamond, the dinner table, and his kids' bedsides. His church and his family both need to see his devotion to parenting, to family. His children need to be more than sermon illustrations; they need to be spoken of warmly and lifted up in front of the church. Of course some kids want to be left out of all sermons, and that's okay too, just so long as the church knows without any doubt that the pastor loves his family more than anything else in the world. This will help alleviate the rivalry between PK and church. (We've already seen how contentious this relationship can be.) It will set a tone in the church of warm fatherhood and commitment to family. It is an example for all to follow. And it is healthiest for all involved.

Consistency: A Positive Trait?

Consistency is nearly synonymous with reliability, and we love being able to rely on people. Such words are seen as good, positive characteristics. They connote trustworthiness and stability, and that is just what we want from a pastor, right? Sure, if he is consistently *good*. Consistency itself is not a thing to be sought after unless what one is consistent in is a benefit.

The reason I bring this up is that it's often seen as a good thing for a pastor to be consistent, the same in his dealings with church members and at home. People often wonder what my dad was like at home. What they are really asking is whether his passionate pulpit persona, strong and pointed views on culture and morals, and intensely rigorous theology are the same when only his family is around. Is he consistent? In short, they want to know if he is a hypocrite.

His ability to be the same in both places is seen as good because it means he's not a hypocrite, and that's what we value about consistency. We want a leader who stands by what he teaches and believes it under all circumstances. But this is about the only way we want consistency. Because what it really means for a pastor to be truly consistent is that his weaknesses are equally obvious in both church and home. Is this what the church wants? Can the church handle it?

At home the pastor might be distant from his kids, unempathetic, or a workaholic. Or maybe he has a temper problem or is harsh to his wife. Maybe he is really poor at listening and relating to his children or he fails to even try. Maybe he sees his role as that of breadwinner and never helps around the house. He can hide these traits at church because the nature of the job keeps him moving from one task to the next, and really he is primarily a preacher, right? The preaching ministry could be flaming brightly while all these other weaknesses are smoldering in the background. Many churches are comfortable with this situation because they are unaware of the dichotomy they have helped establish between home and church.

The kind of consistency the pastor needs—and the kind that is best for his family—is to present himself the same way at the church as at home. This seems impossible. Every family puts on their best face in public and has issues at home nobody knows about, so why should pastors be any different? Because for the church to be a place of healing and safety for sinners and screwups, it needs to be a place of vulnerability and openness, and that comes through leadership— from the pastor.

On the family side, PKs know our parents' sins and failures inside and out, and to see people adore our parents as something they are not ranges from nauseating to heart hardening. I wrote earlier about the necessity of pastors being transparent with their kids—address-ing their own sins, asking for forgiveness, admitting mistakes, being real—and the same is just as important in the church. Everyone in the church must see the pastor's willingness to open up and be real and vulnerable, a sinner. This doesn't mean telling everyone every-thing but rather setting a tone of confession, realness, and honesty as a leader. Pastors cannot let people think something about them that is not true. It is bad for everyone.

When we see our parents consistently put themselves forth as sinners, sinners who do *actual* sins, it helps bridge the gap between pastorate and PK, between church and pastor's family. Each time we see our parents ask for forgiveness from a single church member or the whole congregation, it helps. Each time we see our parents admit a mistake, it helps. And on top of all this, each time we see our parents address head-on the faulty expectations placed on pastors, it helps, because we know they are aware and not acquiescing or embracing.

No Shelter from This Storm

One mistake pastors often make in the relationship between church ministry and family is to try to shelter their kids. I will say as bluntly as I can: This cannot be done. There is no sheltering PKs from pastoral ministry and things going on in the church. Sure, pastors can and ought to keep confidentialities confidential and not overshare with the family. But to try to shelter the PKs from the ministry is to try to live a double life. And it won't work.

Our culture demands nonstop connectedness and work in almost every business. Expectations have changed from jobs being nine to five to something more like "respond immediately to all emails." Smartphones and email keep people plugged in to work all the time. But it doesn't have to be that way. People in most businesses can leave considerable amounts of their work at the office. Craftsmen and artists can leave it in the workshop or studio. Mechanics can leave it at the garage. Nearly anyone who is not on call can, if they really want to, put work away for a while. Not to say any of this is easy. Work has a way of getting into our heads and hearts; it becomes an idol and something by which we identify ourselves. But with discipline, we can push it aside. The same does not hold true for a pastor.

Good pastors have ministry *in* their homes, whether social events, counseling, or housing someone in need. (Of course those pastors who see the home as a place of ministry probably don't see the need to shelter their kids from ministry either.) When ministry crosses the threshold of the home, the parents cannot shelter their kids any longer. Pastoral ministry is ministry of the Word, yes, but it ought to be ministry of relationships too. It's a web of people from staff to elders to deacons to congregants to the community. And this is the same community in which PKs live and socialize and have relationships and conflicts. There is no sheltering them from it.

> "Many pastors feel the need to 'protect' their family
> from the church, rather than lead them in investing
> their lives in it."
>
> —Jon Stepan, PK

No matter how large a buffer pastors try to put between child and church, it's no use. Word gets around. Opinions get shared. People ask questions of PKs about the precise things the pastor was trying to keep from them. Unsolicited feedback on sermons and decisions finds its way to PKs' ears or Facebook pages or Twitter feeds. This is how communities of people work.

The answer isn't to shelter; it is to involve. PKs can't be in on ministry decisions, and I guarantee most don't want to sit in on sermon prep. But pastoral ministry is people ministry, and PKs are in the community of people. So pastors should participate with them and ask questions of them. Issues that arise should be discussed honestly in accordance with the PK's age and awareness, not squelched. When PKs know that questions have been raised or challenges posed—or when they raise those questions themselves—pastors need to address these issues with their children. And at all times, pastors should be honest with their kids about the challenges of people ministry and how sloppy it can get.

Like all slippery areas of parenting, how this is done depends on the child's propensities and preparedness. Pastors must consider their kids' ages and maturity levels before they delve into hard things. But even young kids can be part of many conversations about hard things in the church. Pain and hurt and disappointment will happen, and there is no shelter from it. So pastors should go into it *with* their kids.

Fair Expectations

If there is a double standard for pastors, if there are many things that don't work in the relationship between church, pastor, and PK, what are fair expectations? And what should be expected of whom? In chapter 3 we looked at the unfair expectations for PKs, and we have seen some of the unfair expectations placed on pastors. In this three-way relationship, each member faces different challenges and has different expectations placed on them. And unless all three make significant strides in these areas, the relationship fails to grow out of dysfunction.

The Church

The church—and by this I mean both the church at large and individual local bodies—must ask the right things of its pastors. And it must *not* ask the wrong things. It must stop expecting, either tacitly or explicitly, that pastors will embody perfection in every way. The expectation that pastors be experts in sexuality, finance, organization, leadership, family counseling, building maintenance, music, mental health, and all the other challenges of a church needs to be squelched. Such an expectation feeds the ego of one pastor and crushes the soul of another.

Instead, the church must create an expectation of acceptance. Accept that the pastor is finite and fallible. Accept that he makes mistakes, and accept his admittance of making them. Accept that he does not have time for everyone and he never will. Accept that his family is more important to him than the church members. And more than accepting all of this, the church must make known to him that it is *expected* of him.

The church, whether or not it knows it, does not want a pastor who sees himself as an expert, who is afraid or unable to admit mistakes, and who devotes himself to the church before his family. Instead, it wants a pastor who exhibits his humanity in the pulpit and in relationship, who is real about his weaknesses, and who sets an example of humility in word and deed. This does not mean that he is not a leader. It means he is not a potentate or a CEO. Instead, he is a leader by example, exemplifying repentance, values, morality, grace and the need for it, and love toward all—especially his family. This is what the church wants and needs.

The Pastor

Throughout the first six chapters of the book I have poured out expectations on the pastor, especially in relation to his kids. There is no need to repeat them here. I have also described the cultural, unfair, unbiblical expectations the pastor carries. Much should be expected of pastors—and much of what is so often laid on them should not be expected. Instead of being superinfluencers, they must simply strive to be godly fathers and humble leaders, no matter how difficult it is or how many times they fail.

Just as the church must not expect the wrong things of a pastor, so the pastor must not let the wrong expectations of a church change him. Changing a culture is difficult and takes time; the church will not change quickly. So the pastor must respond with firm conviction, backbone, and steadiness. He must maintain and express his commitment to family and grace. For many pastors, this means they must intentionally make themselves lower in their congregations' eyes. They must declare their humanity and fallibility—not in excess, but in realness. They must act like Paul and Barnabas when the men of Lystra worshipped them as Roman gods. They rushed into the crowd and declared, "Men, why are you doing these things? We also are men, of like nature with you."[13] The pastor must maintain at all times that he is just like his people.

Lastly, the pastor would do well to think of his family's knowledge of him and act in accordance. Do his children know of his temper? Do they see him as faithful to the Word? Do they see him as affectionate to his wife? Or maybe they know of his gossip about church members and griping about leadership committees. A pastor's family is an important litmus test for areas of life needing confession, forgiveness, repentance, and growth as well as areas of health and strength. In short, a pastor's spouse and kids know the real person, and if he chooses to present himself as anything else in the public eye, it creates a rift at home and a rift between family and church.

The PK

As much as there is a burden on churches and pastors to make changes, PKs are not excluded. It is easy to play the victim card and demand that everyone else fix our problems. Yes, the challenges PKs face are real. Yes, many pastors and churches have created hurtful environments for us. But the moment we recognize our difficulties, no matter whose fault they are, we must own them and take steps to change them. This is especially true in a relational context where there are no one-way streets. And it is even truer in a context where all are sinners who have hurt others and all need grace. So what is it that PKs must do rather than wallowing in victimhood?

We must be kind and patient, gracious and forgiving. People do not change quickly. In many cases people struggle to even recognize the parts they played in our difficulties. Church cultures do not change quickly. So there will be ongoing needs and opportunities to forgive. If we fall into bitterness or run out of forgiveness, not only have we failed to be Christlike, we have cut off the chance for repaired relationship. We absolutely cannot give up on grace. God's grace has never run out for us, and so long as we are receiving it, we must give it, no matter how grievous the hurts or aggravating the relationships. We have been forgiven too much to stop forgiving others.

One of the greatest challenges PKs have is being forthright about frustrations and hurts. This isn't because of dishonesty usually but because we don't think people will understand or, at a deeper level, because we haven't been able to sort through what they are. That is part of why I wrote this book—to help PKs make sense of, sort through, and express those bottled-up frustrations and pains.

What happens too often *is* bottling up, suppressing them until we get shaken just enough and the lid blows off and the hurt sprays everywhere. Instead, we must, we *must*, speak of what has made life hard—especially to our parents. These can be miserable conversations. They can hurt our parents, and often our parents don't want to take responsibility or are unable to see the parts they played. But those are not reasons to give up on speaking to them. Such conversations are how healing often begins. They create an opportunity for forgiveness and restoration. And they serve our parents by helping them see what they can grow in. Without our willingness to humbly yet boldly talk about our challenges, no healing can happen at home or in the church.

The last thing PKs must remember is that every church frustrates. Churches are groups of sinful people who believe the same things and are trying to go in the same direction. Such a venture is fraught with mistakes, hurts, stupidity, and frustration. I have been a member of four different churches in my life, and all of them have frustrated me, all for different reasons. There simply isn't a perfect church out there. But this is not a reason to give up on church. Because, despite its ugliness and brokenness, the church is the place where healing happens. Yes, it is also the place where much of our hurt happens, but isn't that just like family? They hurt you and you hurt them and yet you still love them and would do anything for them. The church is our family; it's the family that God gave us, so don't give up on it. There isn't a better place out there in which to be restored.

Chapter 8

PKS: WHAT
ARE THEY
GOOD FOR?

Don't worry. It's not all bad news for PKs. I know it seems like it, and in part that was the point of writing this book—to point out hard things. But I don't believe that PKs are lost causes or that our case is hopeless. The struggles of a PK are not some sort of sentence of doom or tragic self-fulfilling prophecy. No, they are a process. For some PKs, it doesn't have a happy ending, but for many, it is the long and winding road to a place of strong, happy relationship with God and meaningful service showing people Jesus.

I know this is true because of my own story of failures, sin, redemption, failure again, and redemption again, and finally the awareness of a God whose grace is greater than all my sin—and greater than any issues I have from being a PK. I know it is true because of the number of PKs I interacted with during the writing of this book, whose stories are ones of struggle, redemption, and now serving Jesus. And from these stories I have seen three ways that PKs are uniquely blessed.

Biblical Building Blocks

Not every PK has the benefit of parents who emphasize Scripture because, sadly, not every pastor takes God's Word very seriously. But on the whole, PKs are raised in Bible-saturated homes. Earlier in the book I described how such saturation can make the Bible rote and

boring for PKs, and that is true. I described how often PKs disagree
with parents about how to interpret or apply biblical truths. But
neither the roteness nor the disagreements can change one simple
fact: It is always a good thing to know God's Word. And PKs have an
opportunity above and beyond almost anyone else to do this.

The biblical teaching PKs receive in the home provides building
blocks, often ones that we are unaware of. I left home to move from
Minnesota to Illinois to attend Wheaton College at age eighteen.
Wheaton has a long tradition as a staunchly evangelical college with
a firm biblical base. It has produced some of the most significant
evangelical figures of the last century, men such as Billy Graham and
Jim Elliot and former Speaker of the House Dennis Hastert. It has a
reputation as an academically strong institution with a sharp student
body. So I expected to meet a bunch of Bible scholars when I got
there, fellow students who knew their Bibles cover to cover. What
a surprise it was to find out that many of these good Christian kids
raised by godly parents simply didn't know their Bibles that well. It
dawned on me then what a unique opportunity I had growing up to
be immersed in the stories and teachings of the Bible so that, even
though I had miles to go in learning interpretation and theology, I at
least knew what the pages said.

Such building blocks may lie dormant inside us, but the significant thing about the Bible is that it is "living and active," "breathed
out by God."[14] For PKs to be filled with biblical content even when
we are not filled with passion or understanding still puts the pieces
in place for God to build something later. For me, this has been
ongoing. During college I began to see Scripture as something more
than a devotional book: as God's story of redemption. After college

I lost sight of this truth and stumbled in life and made some significant mistakes. It was then when the ugliness and horror of sin stared me in the face and I saw the consequences of walking away from God. I saw how sin hurts people—coworkers, my wife, my children, my friends, my church. It was also when all the realities of forgiveness and grace became real to me. I saw Jesus in a real way, as the sacrificial lamb who died in my place and the great high priest who talks to God on my behalf. The crazy thing is that none of this was new to me! It just became alive. All the knowledge was in there, and then God made it come alive to me. That is the blessing of being immersed in Scripture.

Unique Preparation for Ministry

Ministry doesn't have to refer to pastoral ministry particularly. It could mean working for a parachurch ministry or support ministry (like publishing, where I work), or simply being actively involved in church and community ministry. As I was preparing to write this book, I corresponded with several dozen PKs from around the country, and one of the most surprising things to me was the number who had found their way back into vocational ministry. With all the frustrations of being a PK, one would think they would all flee ministry, but no. Why is this? Because PKs have been given a wealth of preparation for ministry whether or not we know it or wanted it at the time.

We've Seen What Others Haven't

PKs have the catbird seat to pastoral ministry. No, we don't sit in on all the meetings and counseling sessions. But we get to see the pastor in every capacity of ministry in an unprecedented way. Of course most of us aren't thinking about this during our growing-up years. We're just trying to get through life. But along the way we absorb all sorts of lessons and realities through simple observation and proximity.

Our exposure to the ups and downs of ministry makes us much less pie-in-the-sky about ministry. Too many wide-eyed seminarians head into ministry ready to, as the late Chris Farley once eloquently put it, "get the world by the tail and wrap it around and pull it down and put it in my pocket!"[15] Little do they know what struggles and hardships await. This doesn't present as much of a problem for PKs. All of us have seen our parents go through deep waters in the church. We have seen them struggle to survive fractured church leadership and factions in the church. We know ministry can be a bear. Ministry lost the ethereal glow of false expectations a long time ago for PKs. We are less inclined to be surprised at the struggles of those in ministry. After all, we saw the struggles in our own homes.

The flip side to this coin is that we have seen the pleasures of ministry. I don't mean the pleasure of a pastor basking in the praises of a congregation after a particularly good sermon. I mean the pleasures of the little moments—helping mend a broken marriage, praying with a heartbroken widow, serving the destitute man who knocks at the door. I mean the close fellowship of a united church staff or leadership team. I mean the deep, humbling satisfaction of seeing God use faithful ministry over time to right a sinking ship of a church. PKs are privy to this and are absorbing it without realizing it. So when we are given the opportunity to enter into ministry, we know the extremes, we know the tension, and we know the ups and downs. We are more prepared for what will come.

We Have Been (Unwitting and Unwilling) Apprentices

Earlier I discussed the difficulties of relating to God when He is Dad's boss, when God is the job. And while that is true, PKs gain distinct benefits while growing up in a vocational ministry context. It serves as practical preparation for ministry. PKs have had the opportunity to see what it takes to succeed in ministry and what it takes to fail. We have watched our parents lead and seen what works and what does not. We have learned aspects of leadership, both positive and negative.

PKs have the unique opportunity to be exposed to ministry and leaders outside of their own families too. Most pastors drag their families to denominational conventions or pastors' conferences at some point. More common than that is getting together for dinners or having guest preachers over after church. Whether these leaders are prominent and well-known or faithful shepherds of small congregations, they can provide invaluable education.

It happens through books too. Every pastor worth his salt is a reader, and PKs see this and hear the comments made about the books and maybe even pick one up and thumb through it. In all, PKs absorb an enormous amount of ministry philosophy, leadership wisdom, and understanding of truth.

The practical education PKs receive is remarkable. Simply being part of the rhythm of pastoral life is impactful. Seeing how Dad prepares his sermons. Hearing his sermons. Seeing and hearing conversations about everything from politics to necklines to exhaustive divine foreknowledge. Noting how Dad prepares for meetings and what he talks about afterward. Listening to the way vision for the church is discussed and communicated. Hearing what is emphasized as paramount and what is treated as secondary in life and theology. It all adds up to a profound understanding of how ministry works.

Ministry Is People

"The value of seeing people loving Jesus was great. Sitting around after church on a Sunday night and listening to ministers tell funny stories, missionaries paint exotic pictures, and all of them talk about how God was working was a blessing that grew me. Being around these people caused a desire inside me for those things."

—Jeremy Noel, PK

Ministry isn't just about methods and philosophies and practices, though. It is about people. It is a study in people and focused interaction with people. It is the ability to interact with and care for numerous types of people, to empathize with them and understand them. Most people in the church, though, have a limited exposure to the spread of humanity. This isn't any fault of their own; it's just the way life works.

The church is a massive web of complicated relationships between all flavors of broken people. Navigating and untangling it is not easy for anyone going into ministry, especially if they are unaware of what awaits. Newly minted pastors are walking unwittingly into a trap.

Their lack of experience and awareness will leave them blindsided by the attacks, the secrets, the gossip, and the demands. They may struggle to determine who is to be trusted and who is to be depended on. It will be a steep learning curve to be sure.

PKs, though, have the chance to interact with anyone and everyone, to see all the characters in the church community. Through our parents' ministry we have encountered the whole spectrum of church humanity. We know the prayer warriors and the entitled, the committed and the apathetic. We have interacted with the leaders and the followers and the leeches and the servants. We have met the missionaries and the senders. We know the naysayers and the encouragers.

This experience sets us up well for ministry by building a basic awareness of what is to come. We both anticipate the worst and know the goodness that is in the congregation. We are less likely to be blindsided by an attack or some exposed sin. And we are able to sense whom we can lean on and trust in as friends, mentors, and supporters. Of course, this is not infallible, but it is the formation of an instinct that serves PKs well in ministry.

Parents Who Serve Jesus

I have been hard on pastors throughout this book. I have pointed out weaknesses and tendencies and failures. I have prodded and demanded and pushed them to be different, to change, to become aware. But now I want to express thanks. I want to say that PKs are blessed to have parents who devote their lives to serving Jesus. It is a challenging calling, and not one person in the world's history has figured out how to do it perfectly. It is a daunting life. But it is necessary and good and rewarding. So thank you, pastors (and spouses). You have given your lives to serving Jesus and His church, and that is a blessing.

PKs are often at odds with our parents about lifestyle and theological differences. We are aware of their shortcomings. We know their failures. But too often we let these get in the way of something very significant. Good pastors are doing their best to set an example of honoring Jesus with their lives. And that is not something any kid can put a value on. We may choose to live life differently than our parents, but at every point we knew they cared about honoring Jesus. And that is irreplaceable.

Where Does This Leave Us?

Writing this book was hard. Maybe it's more accurate to say that a lot of hardship went into writing this book, some of it in my own family and some of it through the pain of other PKs I connected with along the way. So many PKs carry so much pain and anger and sorrow with them. Some of them have fallen into bitterness, and others are rightly doing the hard work of trusting in Jesus to help them through. It is this latter group that has so encouraged me and can encourage you too. Let me share a story of one PK I know and her journey from church to knowing God.[16]

Callie grew up in a church very similar to my own, a strongly biblical and theologically oriented burgeoning megachurch. Her father was an associate pastor, and her mother was deeply involved in the church's various ministries. Callie's older siblings were good kids, generally obedient, and also heavily involved in the church. Her family was close, and her parents loved her, although they were often overly legalistic and strict.

As she moved into junior high and high school, Callie grew more and more frustrated with the church. The God of her parents held little appeal. All the theology and Bible lessons she knew rang hollow. She couldn't connect with anything in the ministry, and she had nobody to open up to about her struggles. Her parents had their answers set in stone. Her siblings knew what they believed. Callie was lonely and empty.

She threw herself into volleyball year round; it was one place where she found happiness. She dated around but never committed to any one guy and dabbled in the party scene. She kept her friends as close as a phone call but no closer. In high school, Callie's relationship with her mother was deteriorating fast. The only recourse her mom had was to pull the reins harder, reinforce the rules, and remind Callie of the same old theological framework. Callie bucked against it all, even moving in with a friend at one point.

When it came time to select a college, Callie decided three states away was the right distance to move from her mother, and off she went to get far away, devote herself to volleyball, and move on in life. But all that emptiness caught up to her in her first year. She fell apart emotionally. She had no God and no close friends, and all the parties and sports were a poor consolation. After one school year Callie moved to a small Christian college closer to home where she connected with a coach who began to show her what it meant to *know* God, to connect to Jesus. It was just seeds planted at that point, but it was something.

A year later, Callie realized she was still too close to the travails of growing up, so off she went again to another Christian college four hundred miles from home. There she buried herself in volleyball. During this time she met a guy on the men's team named Will, and they started dating. Things were going fine until a serious shoulder injury ended her career. Callie was devastated.

After graduation, Will and Callie married. Some of their friends and family wondered if it was a wise move. It seemed like she was grasping at the first solid thing she could find to anchor herself. During their first couple of years of marriage, Will and Callie moved twice as he climbed the ladder at work. Again she felt like she was empty and drifting. The moves carried her from new lonely place to new lonely place. Their relationship began to fall apart. Will was emotionally distant. Callie didn't even know what she wanted, so she left him. Will knew he wanted to do all he could to save the marriage, and he committed himself to changing, seeking counsel, and working things out. Callie wanted no part in it. She was dry, empty, finished.

On the day they were to meet with lawyers to finalize the divorce, Callie called Will and asked to meet beforehand. During a two-hour conversation, she confessed to him that she knew she was broken and needed God, whatever that meant. She knew she wanted to figure out their marriage, whatever that meant. So just hours before they would have ended their marriage, Will and Callie made the decision to give their marriage to God and see what He could do.

In the years since, God has done an enormous amount. They still struggle. They still have hard times. But when Callie talks about God now, she talks about a God she knows. When she describes what Jesus means to her, she talks about a friend. Will is changing too, as the Spirit is opening his heart and softening him. Callie has even come to a place of understanding with her mother. They might never see eye to eye on certain things, but it is a relationship of respect and love, one where Mom is learning to see that Callie loves Jesus and follows God even if it doesn't look exactly the way Mom wants.

I tell you this story because it is so amazing and so amazingly normal. Girl grows up a PK, is disillusioned with the church, doesn't know God, tries to make her own way, and falls apart. But God's grace is bigger than all that disillusionment and is powerful enough to open the eyes of Callie's heart to Him. It is big enough for you and me too.

PKs face many challenges that are unique to the nature of our families. Every pastor's family is different—some are utterly dysfunctional, while others are quite healthy, with all manner of families in between. Not everything I have written applies to every PK, and some PKs face struggles I did not address. I hope that as you continue to reflect on the challenges, you will increasingly see ways to change. The church, the pastor, and the PK all have our work cut out. The church needs to create a more hospitable environment for PKs (and pastors). Pastors need to be aware of their children's struggles and take the necessary steps to create supportive, safe, strong, open spaces for them. PKs, despite all these struggles, cannot wallow in and bemoan them. Rather, we must own what responsibilities are ours: to honor Jesus, to honor our fathers and mothers, to love and support the church, and to go about our lives not as victims but as the redeemed. Grace is here for all of us.

Appendix

SEVEN RULES FOR WHEN YOU MEET A PK

1. Do not ask us "What is it like to be the son or daughter of …?"

How are we supposed to answer that question? Could you easily describe being the child of your parents? Remember, PKs are normal people with just a different upbringing than you. Please treat us that way. We think of our parents as parents, nothing more.

2. Do not quote our dads to us.

This is really and truly annoying because it comes across as one of two things. Either you are proving your piousness by being so aware of the utterances of the beloved pastor, or you are being condescending and holding our parents' words over our heads. Neither is impressive or appreciated.

3. Do not ask us anything personal you would not ask of anyone else.

If, perchance, you have gained some knowledge of a PK through a sermon illustration or book or hearsay, it is best to keep it to yourself. To ask a question based on knowledge that you gained in an impersonal manner makes you look like either a stalker or a reporter. Both are creepy.

4. Do not ask us anything about our dads' positions on anything.

"What does your dad think about …?" is a question no PK wants to answer—not about politics, the roles of women in the church, predestination, the use of drums in the worship service, spiritual gifts, race, or anything else. We have opinions and beliefs, though. And we like to converse. So you could ask us what we think, like a normal person.

5. Do not assume you can gain audience with the pastor through us.

That's what the church secretary or the pastor's assistant is for. Please let us be his children. We usually don't have the ability to make a meeting happen, and we almost never want to.

6. Do not assume that we agree with all the utterances of our fathers.

I know it's hard to believe that any child could grow up to disagree with her parents, but it does happen. It is not kind or safe to assume that our parents' positions are ours. And when you find out we don't agree, please refrain from being shocked or offended.

7. Get to know us.

This is a good rule for anyone, but it especially pertains to PKs. Just as you want people to value your opinions, personality, and character quirks, so do we. More often than not you will get a surprise. Wow, that PK actually has a sense of humor! Who knew PKs could be so fun? Wait, he said what? Leave your assumptions at the door and let us be us. You'll probably like what you find.

NOTES

1. Two great books on the subject of young people leaving the faith are *UnChristian: What a New Generation Really Thinks about Christianity … and Why It Matters*, by Dave Kinnaman and Gabe Lyons (Baker, 2007); and *Generation Ex-Christian: Why Young Adults Are Leaving the Faith … and How to Bring Them Back*, by Drew Dyck (Moody, 2010).

2. You can hear the sermon at Desiring God's website: www.desiringgod.org/resource-library/conference-messages/doing-missions-when-dying-is-gain.

3. In the movie *A Christmas Story*, the young character Flick is "triple dog dared" to lick a frozen metal pole. In the code of boyhood, this is a dare that cannot be turned down. You'll have to watch the movie to see how it turns out.

4. For a helpful primer on Calvinistic theology, read *The Doctrines of Grace: Rediscovering the Evangelical Gospel*, by James Boice and Philip Ryken (Crossway Books, 2009).

5. Complementarianism states that God created men and women with distinct roles. They are separate but equal. It takes seriously the role of man as the head of the household and the biblical teaching that only men should be pastors and elders in the church. This doctrine has a broad range of application, but those are the key tenets.

6. Paedobaptists are those who believe in and practice the baptizing of infants. Protestant denominations that practice it include Presbyterians, Lutherans, Methodists, Anglicans, Episcopalians, and others.

7. My editor's exact words about this phrase are that it is "a somewhat archaic expression that comes from Acts 10:34 (KJV).... Nobody but pastors and their kids (and the occasional editor) knows what it means."

8. In this 1994 film, Tim Robbins plays Andy Dufresne, a successful banker falsely imprisoned for murder. Morgan Freeman plays Red, another inmate who befriends Andy. It is a remarkable story of perseverance, survival, and justice.

9. For a wonderful, full look at the theology of work and calling, read Tim Keller's *Every Good Endeavor: Connecting Your Work to God's Work* (Dutton, 2012).

10. A 2010 LifeWay survey of more than 1,000 pastors found that over 65 percent of pastors worked more than 50 hours per week. Eight percent admitted to working more than 70 hours. It can be difficult for pastors to accurately gauge their work hours because of the fuzzy lines between such activities as personal study and sermon preparation or meeting with someone and having a meeting. For more on the data, see Mark Kelly, "LifeWay Research Finds Pastors' Long Work Hours Come at Expense of People, Ministry," LifeWay, January 5, 2010, accessed July 27, 2013, www.lifeway.com/Article/ LifeWay-Research-finds-pastors-long-work-hours-can-come-at-the-expense-of-people-ministry.

11. Rainer blogged about the survey and his thoughts on the findings in "How Many Hours Must a Pastor Work to Satisfy the Congregation?," Thomrainer.com, July 24, 2013, accessed July 27, 2013, http://thomrainer.com/2013/07/24/how-many-hours-must-a-pastor-work-to-satisfy-the-congregation/.

12. Darryl Dash, "How Many Hours Should Pastors Work?," Dashhouse.com, March 21, 2013, accessed July 27, 2013, http://dashhouse.com/dashhouse/2013/3/21/how-many-hours-should-pastors-work.

13. Acts 14:15.

14. Hebrews 4:12; 2 Timothy 3:16.

15. Quoted from Farley's famous "Matt Foley: Motivational Speaker" *Saturday Night Live* skit.

16. Names and details changed to protect the subjects' privacy.

ACKNOWLEDGMENTS

I offer my deepest thanks to my wife, Lesley. Your encouragement and strong insistence that I write this book and your belief in my message spurred me along the way. Your constant efforts to make time in our busy life for me to write made completing this book easy. Thank you for helping and pushing me so much. You are the structure and strength that get my ideas down on paper.

Thank you to Alex Field for being excited about this project from our first conversation at the Catalyst conference in 2012 and for championing it at David C Cook. As a first-time author, having a publisher who actively wanted what I wrote was an enormous boon.

Thank you to the team at David C Cook who have worked so diligently and been so accessible and helpful in the improvement and publication of this book. You have been a pleasure to work with and have truly taken my work and made it better.